RELIGION & AGING

an annotated bibliography

RELIGION & AGING

an annotated bibliography

COMPILED BY

VINCENT JOHN FECHER

TRINITY UNIVERSITY PRESS
San Antonio, Texas

© Copyright Vincent John Fecher 1982
Library of Congress Catalog Card Number 82-81019
ISBN 0-911536-96-5 cloth
ISBN 0-911536-97-3 paper
Printed by Best Printing Company
Bound by Custom Bookbinders
Manufactured in the United States of America

Trinity University Press, San Antonio, Texas 78284

FOREWORD

Those who wish to understand and respond to changes concomitant with the aging process must examine carefully the various dimensions of physical, mental, social, and spiritual health. As we age, our biological systems, which begin to slow down in late adolescence, continue to decline gradually. Psychologically, we must learn to adapt to living with fewer friends and confidants—those persons who reinforce and validate who we are. Our social world becomes smaller and smaller and spiritually we begin to contemplate, once and for all, the meaning of life itself. In essence, as we pass through each phase of the life cycle our general welfare changes significantly. Appropriate answers to the many questions that emerge from this experience require our thoughtful consideration. Indeed, to encounter the full drama of life and interpret its meanings within the context of our religious faith is a challenge which, ultimately, faces us all.

While aging studies traditionally have encompassed a wide range of academic and applied fields, only recently has the spiritual dimension been recognized as essential to a complete understanding of personhood across the lifespan. In the last ten years, a growing number of professionals, paraprofessionals, academicians, ministers, and laypersons have begun to explore the phenomenon of aging within the context of religious faith. Moreover, an increasing number of social and behavioral scientists are incorporating religious-related variables in their research designs and methodologies. Current holistic models of health care as well as preventive medicine and hospice approaches to care include religious faith as a significant component of treatment and rehabilitation. In short, although the fields of sociology, psychology, and biology continue to shape the course of gerontological studies, contributions from theology and religion are providing a dimension which fills the gaps and helps to create a more mature understanding of the aging process.

Through his comprehensive research in this area, Vincent Fecher has made a substantial contribution to the pursuit of a more holistic image of growing older. The 500 or more references in this volume are unprecedented. Moreover, this bibliography provides a central resource at a time when the consolidation of existing scholarly and other work is acutely needed. Gerontology is indeed enriched by Fecher's investigation into the emerging field of religion and aging.

David B. Oliver
Kansas City, Missouri

ACKNOWLEDGMENTS

May I hereby express my deepest appreciation to all who aided me with this project in any way. Particular thanks are due to Dr. David Oliver, who initially encouraged the idea of compiling an annotated bibliography of religion and aging; to Dr. Charles White, whose interest and approval made it my master's project; to Mrs. Norma Carmack of the Trinity University Library for her help in planning a computer search of the literature; to Mrs. Katherine Pettit of Trinity University Library, whose valiant efforts procured much hard-to-find material through interlibrary loan. Finally, a word of appreciation is also due for the cheerful cooperation of many librarians in Texas and in Washington, D.C., and to the editors of journals who promptly replied to my requests for material that was published years ago, but which was for some reason unobtainable through the usual channels. To all of them, a hearty *Vergelt's Gott!*

CONTENTS

FOREWORD BY DAVID B. OLIVER, Poppele Chair,
Saint Paul School of Theology, Kansas City, Missouri • v

Acknowledgments • vi

INTRODUCTION: ABOUT THIS BIBLIOGRAPHY • 3

I. THE RELIGION OF THE ELDERLY • 9

II. ORGANIZED RELIGION IN THE SERVICE OF THE ELDERLY • 35

III. SPIRITUAL MINISTRATION TO THE ELDERLY • 61

IV. MISCELLANEOUS TITLES ON RELIGION AND AGING • 85

SUPPLEMENT: TITLES WITHOUT ANNOTATION • 113

INDEX

    SUBJECT • 115

    AUTHOR • 117

RELIGION & AGING

an annotated bibliography

INTRODUCTION
ABOUT THIS BIBLIOGRAPHY

This bibliography of works about religion and aging differs in several respects from its predecessors in the field. For one thing, it contains 473 annotated entries. That alone makes it four times larger than the most ambitious religion-and-aging bibliography published to date (Cook, 1976). Secondly, this listing has been done by one individual, who personally examined each work and made an independent summary of its contents.

There is a third difference. In the pages that follow, we are looking only at those writings which deal with the *interaction* of religion and aging, or with the impact of the one upon the other. In modern jargon, we are concerned with the "interface" of religion and aging though I personally prefer to think of all these studies as so many points along the line where the two planes of religion and aging intersect. Such a focus sets this effort apart from a number of other bibliographies which at first sight seem to cover the same area (for instance, Morgan, 1977; Vega, 1979), but where other material is included about aging per se, on the theory (stated or implied) that information of this type will be helpful to religious persons working with the aged.

Defining the Terms

The criterion then is that any work included in this bibliography must somehow involve both the religious and the aging dimensions. Obviously, such a norm necessitates some prior decision on what the terms "religion" and "aging" will mean in the present context.

1. The term "aging" is used in its gerontological sense, referring to that phase in the life cycle when society judges a person to be aged, old, or elderly (for convenience, past 60 or 65 years). I am not concerned here with a developmental concept of aging, which connotes simple maturation with the passing of time. This latter sense of the word is employed when young people are said to be "aging" as they pass from their fourteenth to their twentieth year, for example.

2. The term "religion" is more difficult to define because it means so many different things to different people. Even the experts at the 1971 White House Conference on Aging seem to have had problems, since the upshot of their efforts was such a nebulous phrase—"spiritual well-being"—surely broad enough to cover a multitude of feelings.

One factor that might lead toward a definition would be to distinguish "organized religion" from "personal religion." Then, within the sphere of one's personal religion, one might further distinguish *external practice* (such as institutional membership and attendance) from *the more inward and intimate realm* of one's belief in God, with all the attitudes and practices (such as praying) which might flow from one's beliefs.

Unfortunately, there has been little rigorous scientific research into the inner religious world of older people. Are there really any changes taking place, religiously speaking, in the older years? If so, what are they and to what can they be ascribed—aging, cohort, time of measurement?

There is some literature on the inward religion of the elderly, most of which is nonscientific, with few attempts at scholarly studies. It is generally agreed, however, that the latter have been spotty, inconclusive, and even contradictory. The real work remains to be done.

For that matter, even the sphere of external practice has not been studied thoroughly, though it is more readily observable and quantifiable. Around the middle of our century, there was some show of interest in the subject of church attendance; currently, however, the analysis of churchgoing patterns has been practically abandoned by religious sociologists.

In contrast, there is a much richer literature on the relation of organized religion to the elderly. One is tempted to say that the more relevant question here is not, do the aged go to the churches or the synagogues? but rather, how do the churches or synagogues go to the aged? Nevertheless, in classifying efforts of this kind, I have preferred to avoid such a term as "church" in favor of the term "organized religion" borrowed from Scudder (1958). Being a broader designation, it can include those organizations which draw their inspiration from religion without being a "church" in any strict sense of the word, such as a religious club, an order of nuns, or a wide-spread lay federation. Most literature on programs fits under this heading.

A final word about the understanding of the term "religion" as it is used in organizing this bibliography: It does not include death-and-dying. Two main reasons motivated the exclusion of a burgeoning literature on this topic: one, it is really quite a different matter (there is nothing specifically religious about dying); two, there has been such an explosion of writings about death-and-dying that it would seem to merit a bibliography all its own. If included here, it would only have diluted the explicit focus on religion and aging.

Divisions of the Bibliography

The foregoing distinctions, which explain the term "religion" in the title, already adumbrate the major divisions of our work.

At an early stage in my research, I had planned to list in two separate sections: (a) the literature on external religious observance in the latter years; and (b) the literature on the internal religious beliefs and attitudes of the aged. Since both sections proved to be so small, taken singly, they were eventually combined into one block and called "the religion of the elderly." That is now the first section of the bibliography.

The next section is made up substantially of programs and other efforts of organized religion on behalf of the elderly. Also included are the official policy statements of religious groups and special issues (or numbers) of religious-sponsored periodicals. These statements and special numbers not only demonstrate that organized religion is interested in the aged, but, understood as advocacy, they are "efforts on behalf of the elderly."

By and large, reports on programs and other initiatives to which section II of this bibliography refers (Organized Religion in the Service of the Elderly) record what actually has worked in dealings with older people. Others may find in these pages a ready resource of ideas for grass-roots practitioners who are looking for something that a religious group could do for the elderly. It is hoped that this bibliography, especially in section II, will prove helpful to those in search of suggestions.

Section III, Spiritual Ministration to the Elderly, is devoted to ministry and to resources for leaders of organized religion in their efforts. Whereas section II was concerned with the *temporal* aspects of what organized religion might offer the elderly, section III focuses on the person's *spiritual* or inward well-being, that is, the elderly in relation to God, insofar as such a relationship may be promoted and aided by ministry. Just as section II could provide ideas for those planning programs for the aged under religious auspices, section III may too prove useful in providing ministers with materials to use in their spiritual ministrations with older persons. Therefore, certain biblical and other religious considerations have been included.

On the other hand, I have purposely excluded from section III so-called armchair reflections on the aging problem, which sometimes take the form of a pious exhortation to the religious groups to be up and doing in response to the multiplication of hoary heads in the land, a pastoral problem of huge dimensions. Reflections and exhortations of this type have a certain value, if only as a historical testimony of awareness. I have therefore included some in the "miscellaneous" section.

Inevitably, there will always be a miscellaneous category in any typology, even one that classifies literary and scientific works. In this case, it could have been broken down into a number of subclasses, one of which has just been mentioned. Another could have been formed of the twenty-odd studies concerning the retirement problems of elderly Catholic priests and nuns, and a third could contain the proceedings of conferences, congresses, and meetings, such as the White House Conferences on the Aging. Others, finally, would probably defy any attempt at classification. In the end, to avoid a pointless fragmentation which would only make the bibliography hard to use, it was decided to combine all the minicategories into one general class, comparable in size to the other three. The subject index at the end of the book will aid in selecting from such a combination of topics the ones relevant to the user of this checklist.

Genesis of this Annotated Bibliography

A start was made in the summer of 1979, combing the ongoing bibliography of Dr. Nathan Shock in the *Journal of Gerontology* for any titles that seemed to bear on the interrelation of religion and aging. Subsequently, a similar search was conducted through the various volumes of *Religion Index One: Periodicals* (formerly called *Index to Religious Periodical Literature*), the *Catholic Periodical and Literature Index,* and the National Council on the Aging's quarterly *Current Literature on Aging.* A computer search was run on data stored by Bibliographic Retrieval Services, Inc., with additional material from the National Institute of Mental Health (1969-79). Other bibliographies and indices were consulted such as *Psychological Abstracts* and *Dissertation Abstracts International* and, of course, the bibliographies which were discovered during the research.

Locating the actual books and articles, once I had their titles, was the major part of the undertaking, since I did not want to rely on secondhand information about any publication. The search led in San Antonio through the libraries of Assumption Seminary, Brook Army Medical Center, Incarnate Word College, Oblate College of the Southwest, Our Lady of the Lake University, Trinity University, St. Mary's University, and the University of Texas Health Science Center; in Austin, the library of the University of Texas; and in Washington, D.C., the Library of Congress, the National Council on the Aging, the headquarters of the American Association of Retired Persons, and the Catholic University of America. A number of titles not found in any of the above were successfully tracked down through private correspondence and through interlibrary loan.

Despite all these efforts, some titles remained simply what the French call *introuvable*—they just could not be found. These few are listed in a supplement with no annotations. Information on their whereabouts will be greatly appreciated and will be included (with due acknowledgment) in any revision of the present work, as will errors of fact or judgment for which evidence is presented.

Once the article or book was in hand, an effort was made to produce a summary or descriptive note which would faithfully reflect the contents. In this I tried to take the viewpoint of one who might turn to the bibliography in search of a specific kind of information. Ideally, the reader should be able to tell, on the basis of the note, whether or not the original article might have the material for which he or she is searching. And yet, in drawing up a precis, no procrustean bed was, or even could be, applied. For a collection of scientific papers, delivered by various speakers at a conference or meeting, it seemed that our purpose was best served by simply listing the names of the speakers and the titles of their learned papers. When a book or an article contained a number of subheadings or chapter titles, these titles seemed to offer the best insight into the contents. At times the summary furnished by the journal itself seemed best suited to report on the writer's purpose and findings. However, often it was necessary to rephrase such a precis, with some slight addition or omission based on the actual text of the article. Finally, wherever an original summary was written, an attempt was made to paraphrase the author's own words. And though the thrust was towards descriptive rather than critical notes, there were times when I added a brief evaluation.

Thus, from the outset, there was no intention of adhering to any rigid format in the annotations or notes. The intention was, nevertheless, to be uniform in citing the bibliographical data: periodical, year, volume number, pages, although the periodicals did not always lend themselves to uniform description. Some run the pagination successively through an entire volume or year; others begin each issue of the quarterly or monthly all over again from page 1. To cite both volume *and* number was impossible in those cases where librarians or binderies had removed covers and tables of contents from individual numbers before binding them as one volume. In the end, the goal was to give sufficient data in the bibliographical entries to guide the searcher to the right page.

A word about the few foreign-language entries included in this listing. I did not make an exhaustive search through French, German, Italian, and Spanish literature on religion and aging. Included are only those titles that were in American bibliographies and were available in the United States. In each case, the translation of the foreign title and of the contents for the annotations is mine.

It was beyond the scope of this particular project to research the more general magazines of the various groups, in which stories of projects or personalities often treat the aged. These offer rich fields for further research.

A Final Word on the State of the Literature

I have indicated already my regret that so little has been done to study the inner religious world of the aging person. Even the external religious practice of such people has not been widely and systematically examined.

Organized religion admittedly could be, and should be, doing more for so-called senior citizens. But even on the basis of that *portion* of the total effort that has been reported in section II, one is led to wonder about charges of neglect leveled at "the churches" by certain writers, some of whose essays are in section IV. Religious groups either suddenly began doing more for the aged as a result of these exhortations, or the writers themselves were unaware of what the churches actually were doing. Whichever might be the case, there is a promising field of research for someone's dissertation or monograph concerning organized religion's service to the elderly in the third quarter of the twentieth century.

That there is already a growing body of literature on the subject of religion and aging, this bibliography will testify. The quality of this literature, as might be expected, is rather uneven. It is not the part of the bibliographer to commend or criticize this quality; the compiler's task is only to lead the researcher to the sources.

I. THE RELIGION OF THE ELDERLY

1. Adams, Davis L. Correlates of satisfaction among the elderly. *Gerontologist*, 1971, *11* (4, pt. 2), 64-68.

Different researchers have different ideas about what individual well-being is and how to measure it, hence the somewhat contradictory findings in the literature. This writer reviews the biological, psychological, and sociological correlates of satisfaction among the elderly. Although religion is not mentioned, "belief in afterlife" is included among the psychological ones. The NICA bibliography lists this article as one of the works on religion and aging, probably because such a belief usually is bound up with a person's religion.

2. Albrecht, Ruth E. The meaning of religion to older people — the social aspect. In Scudder, Delton L. (Ed.), *Organized religion and the older person.* Gainesville: Univ. of Florida Press, 1958, 53-70.

This survey is concerned with the social aspects of religious practice, in the light of information obtained through other studies and considering the life-cycle picture as well as patterns found in various social status groups. Subheadings: A Survey of the Situation (including church membership and church attendance); Family Life-Cycle Church Attendance Practices; Social Status Differences; Various Status Groups, Considered Individually: Upper, Upper Middle, etc.; Other Related Factors; Summary.

3. Amen, Sister M. Ann SSJ. Informal groups and institutional adjustments in a Catholic home for the aging. *Journal of Gerontology*, 1959, *14*, 338-43.

A study of 120 residents in a Catholic home for the aged determined how their participation in informal groups is related to their individual adjustment. Eighty-four said that they spent more time on religious activities since coming to the home; 10, about the same amount of time; 11, less. More free time and the proximity of the chapel accounted for the increase in their religious activities.

4. Angus, Jack Duane. Social aspects of aging Catholics of the South Bend Indiana Deanery. *Dissertation Abstracts*, March 1968, 28 (9-A), 3773.

A social survey of a sample of Catholics aged 65 and over, listed on the rolls of 28 parishes in the South Bend Deanery of the Fort Wayne — South Bend Diocese. The universe consisted of 3,695 names, the sample of 928 persons, 745 of whom were interviewed in Nov./Dec. 1960. Areas of concern in the study included health, income, religion, life views, political activity. There was no evidence for a decline in religious life, as measured by Mass attendance: fifteen to twenty percent reported a less-than-weekly attendance, and these attributed the fact largely to poor health. (University of Notre Dame, 1967.)

5. Apfeldorf, Max. Religious belief, emotional adjustment, and constructive ward behavior in the elderly patient during the period of reduced life expectancy: Research plans. *Journal of Thanatology*, 1975, *3*, 113-41.

A team of investigators working on the relationship of religious belief to dying studied six factors: (a) an estimate of limited life expectancy based on the severity of disease; (b) the patient's awareness that one's life expectancy was so limited; (c) an index of intellectual level; (d) a measure of ward behavior and attitudes; (e) religious commitment broadly measured in terms of beliefs and behavior; (f) emotional adjustment. This paper, delivered in 1972 but not printed until 1975, gives no results, although the final paragraphs described plans for examining emphysema patients. No indication was given why this particular disease was chosen as producing awareness of limited life expectancy. A twenty-one page appendix reproduced the questionnaires with questions concerning religious belief and behavior.

6. Bahr, Howard M. Aging and religious disaffiliation. *Social Forces*, 1970, *49*, 59-71.

Comparison between lifetime church attendance patterns of skid-row men and of two so-called normal samples. All showed considerable religious disaffiliation during adult life. With advancing age, both the poor and the well-to-do considered church attendance less important. On the basis of these findings, the author questions some generalizations about church attendance and aging.

7. Barron, Milton L. The role of religion and religious institutions in creating the milieu of older people. In Scudder, Delton L. (Ed.), *Organized religion and the older person.* Gainesville: Univ. of Florida Press, 1958, 12-33.

The purpose of this paper is to investigate the etiological relationship between religion as an independent variable and aging as a dependent variable. Subheadings are: The Theology of Religion and Aging; Religiosity of Older People; Religion and Adjustment in Old Age; Shortcomings of Religion as a Geriatric Factor, Further Research. Five full-page tables on the relationship of chronological age to various religious factors report data from a New York City sample of 496 cases in 1957.

8. Basset, Joseph A. Outside the moat. *Harvard Divinity Bulletin n.s.*, Autumn, 1968, *2*, 16-17.

In small towns 50 to 75 miles outside the metropolitan area, the church is encountering challenges, especially with regard to a sense of community. If older people raise their own theologically significant questions, no one in the church has time to listen. There are obstacles to a "prophetic" type of minister: federal programs are urban-based, and social action is in the hands of an outside expert.

9. Beard, Belle B. Longevity and religiosity: Attitudes and activities of centenarians. *Gerontologist*, Autumn, 1968, 8 (3, pt. 2), 31.

As one phase of a comprehensive study of men and women 100 years old and older, more than a thousand were interviewed on various attitudes concerning religion and afterlife, as well as on such behavior patterns as church attendance, Bible reading, and prayer. The study also sought an answer to questions such as whether people become more religious as they grow older. Data on these thousand centenarians were compared with those obtained from younger age groups and from two other samples of very old people who were not yet centenarians.

10. Beard, Belle B. Religion at one hundred. *Modern Maturity*, June-July, 1969, *12* (3), 57-59.

The researcher asked 700 men and women, 100 years of age or older, about their religious practices and attitudes. More than 90% said that religion was very important to them. Although the writer kept detailed records on how often they prayed, attended services, read the Bible, etc., her data are not presented here in academic fashion because of the nature of the publication. A popularly written article, rich in anecdotal material.

11. Becker, K. F. Religiosität im Alter. *Zeitschrift für Gerontologie*, Jan.-Feb. 1977, *10* (1), 1-2.

Introductory editorial, "Religiosity in old age," to a special number of Z.f.G. (Band 10, Heft 1, Jan.-Feb. 1977) dedicated to the subject of religion and aging. The articles were all written by professional Protestant theologians with a view to promoting interdisciplinary dialogue.

12. Bell, Tony. The relationship between social involvement and feeling old among residents of homes for the aged. *Journal of Gerontology*, 1967, *22*, 17-22.

The sample consisted of 55 residents in two homes for the aged and one senior center. Indices of social involvement were taken from Cumming and Henry. Findings: low social involvement (also in church affairs) was associated with feeling old; high social involvement, feeling not so old.

13. Berardo, Felix M. *Social adaptation to widowhood among a rural-urban aged population.* (Washington State University College of Agriculture Bulletin No. 689.) Pullman, Wash.: Washington Agricultural Experiment Station, 1967, 31.

This study evaluates the social adaptation of aged widows living in the city, in a small town, and in rural areas. One section is on social isolation and participation; in this context, it is found that widows are more active in the church than widowers.

14. Bild, Bernice, & Havighurst, Robert. Senior citizens in great cities: The case of Chicago. *Gerontologist*, 2 Feb. 1976, *16* (1, pt. 2), 1-88.

This is a report sponsored by the Chicago Mayor's Office for Senior Citizens that builds on the first broad "needs assessment" of 1972. Studies were made of several "groups" of elderly persons because it was believed that many of Chicago's "groups" had needs and characteristics differing from those of other groups. The religious differential seems to have received little attention: religion is given a passing mention on page 25.

15. Blazer, Dan G., & Palmore, Erdman. Religion and aging: An analysis of a longitudinal panel. *Gerontologist*, 1975, *15* (5, pt. 2), 68.

The sample consisted of 260 elderly persons, mostly Protestant, studied in 1955. Survivors were checked at nine points of time up to the date of this paper, which was presented at the scientific meeting of the Gerontological Society in October 1975. Of the subjects studied, 94% were church members, and these had a wide range of activities and interests. Their over-all religious level remained constant throughout the twenty years covered by the study. Though religion seemed to have little effect on happiness and later-life adjustment, it did correlate positively with a feeling of usefulness.

16. Blazer, Dan G., & Palmore, Erdman. Religion and aging in a longitudinal panel. *Gerontologist*, 1976, *16* (1), 82-85.

Data examined in this study were collected in Duke University's first longitudinal study of aging (Palmore, 1970, 1974). The original longitudinal sample was composed of 272 volunteers, all from the Durham area. The age range was 60 to 94 years, with a median age of 70.8; 90% were Protestant, 94% were church members. Religious activities were relatively frequent and showed a gradual increase over time. Religious attitudes remained stable; they were not significantly related to happiness and only slightly related to adjustment.

17. Bortner, Rayman W., & Hultsch, David F. A multivariate analysis of correlates of life satisfaction in adulthood. *Journal of Gerontology*, 1970, *25*, 41-47.

Religion was included as one of the "social psychological variables"; the question asked was, "How important is religion in your life?" A multiple regression analysis yielded a significant correlation between life satisfaction and 27 independent variables (religion among them). The aged were included in this study, though it was not limited to them.

18. Bower, Janet. *Older People of St. Boniface Parish.* Buffalo, New York: Catholic Charities of Buffalo, 1957.

St. Boniface is an old, predominantly German parish in the "Fruit Belt" section of the city of Buffalo. The study group consisted of 262 parish members 60 years of age and over, though only 238 could be interviewed.

The questionnaire on which the interviews were based is reproduced in Appendix B (pp. 95-104). It covers eight areas: (1) neighbor relations; (2) housing; (3) family; (4) health; (5) work; (6) finances; (7) interests; (8) religion. The findings of the study are summarized in 119 tables which span pages 11 through 89. These are followed by "recommendations" (90-92).

19. Brennan, Constance L., & Missinne, Leo E. Personal and institutionalized religiosity of the elderly. In Thorson, James A., & Cook, Thomas C., Jr. (Eds.), *Spiritual well-being of the elderly*. Springfield, Ill.: Charles C. Thomas, 1980, 92-99.

This project sought to determine how important the individual saw religion as being in his or her life, as well as any changes perceived in belief or participation as the individual had aged. A total of 92 persons ranging in age from 59 to 93 years answered the questionnaire reproduced on page 96. Results supported the hypothesis that religious feelings and activities remain fairly constant throughout adult life.

20. Brown, Philip S. Religious needs of older persons. In Thorson, James A., & Cook, Thomas C., Jr. (Eds.), *Spiritual well-being of the elderly*. Springfield, Ill.: Charles C. Thomas, 1980, 76-82.

The older person is concerned about answers to such questions as, "Who am I? What is my purpose? Where am I going?" Religion must address itself to these issues. Four possible world views are presented, ranging from atheism to pantheism.

21. Browning, Don S. Preface to a practical theology of aging. *Pastoral Psychology*, Winter, 1975, *24* (229), 151-67. NB: Also found on 151-67 of Hiltner, Seward (Ed.), *Toward a theology of aging*. New York: Human Sciences Press, 1975, 181.

A practical theology of aging must use phenomenological description and empirical analysis to open up the surface and the depth dimensions of experience. The results must be correlated with the hermeneutics of Christian symbols. The key to meaningful aging will then emerge as learning to "care" for oneself, for one's future, and the future of the race.

22. Buesching, Sister Rosaria. Successful aging: A religious viewpoint. In Bier, William C. (Ed.), *Aging: Its challenge to the individual and to society*. New York: Fordham University Press, 1974, 282-92.

The correlation of religious development with human development and the contribution of religion to one's later years.

23. Catholic Digest Survey. Do Americans believe in God? *Catholic Digest*, Nov. 1952, *17*, 1-5.

An extensive scientific survey, of which question 10-a was, "Do you believe in God?" The table on page 4 analyzes the answers according to many categories, one of which is age. In the 65-and-over age bracket, 91% were "absolutely certain" and a further 7% were "fairly sure."

24. Catholic Digest Survey. Do Americans go to church? *Catholic Digest*, Dec. 1952, *17*, 1-7.

In the table on page 5, Attendance at Sunday Church, it appears that 42% of the 65-and-over bracket never attend, while 31% attend every Sunday or Sabbath, and 22% (in the table, 8 plus 14%) attend two or three times a month.

25. Catholic Digest Survey. How important religion is to Americans. *Catholic Digest*, Feb. 1953, *17*, 6-12.

The table on page 8 shows that of those 65 and over, 84% considered religion "very important" in their own lives; 11% would call it "fairly important." Only 4% found it "not very important."

26. Christiansen, Drew. Dignity in aging: Notes on geriatric ethics. *Journal of Humanistic Psychology*, 1978, *18* (2), 41-54.

A criticism of Goffman's idea of *dignity* and *person*. The term *dignity* can have several distinct meanings: normative concept, social behavior, inner strength and freedom towards events. The aged suffer a loss of dignity through social diminishment, the boredom of the young with old people's talk. Dignity and its devices: Defiance and Self-Respect, Interdependence, Serenity, The Importance of Recognition, Loss and Indignity, Submission, Indifference, The Hindu Example.

27. Clingan, Donald. *Let your light shine!* Indianapolis: Christian Theological Seminary, 1978.

A report on a "field project in ministry" done for a Doctor of Ministry degree, this bit of research attempted to measure "the impact of one-day older adult retreats and a twelve-week small group experience on older persons." The conclusion: the one-day older adult retreats did not bring about the same kind of life changes that had been generated by a twelve-week, life-enrichment small group for older adults.

28. Cole, Elbert. Spiritual and religious dimensions of aging: Applications. In Thorson, James A., & Cook, Thomas C., Jr. (Eds.), *Spiritual well-being of the elderly.* Springfield, Ill.: Charles C. Thomas, 1980, 214-17.

Older people are asking, "What is the meaning and purpose of life?" This is a religious question. The religious and spiritual sectors of the community must be challenged. The fundamental talk in our society is not political, but religious.

29. Collier, Charlotte Meier. A community study of aging and religion among rural Pennsylvania Germans. *Dissertation Abstracts International*, February 1979, *39* (8-A), 5012.

(Citation 29 continued)

The study population, located in a rural-urban fringe township of Southeastern Pennsylvania, is predominantly German Protestant—Anabaptist, Lutheran, and Reformed. It comprised 164 people aged 65 and over, 63 men and 101 women. Tools of research included an interview schedule, participant observation, key-informant interviews, written records, and questionnaires. Two main findings were, that older people in the research population related to the community, to one another, and to the aging experience through their religion; and that older people in this research population were vital, participating, and integrated members of the community. (University of Massachusetts, 1978.)

30. Cook, John William. An application of the disengagement theory of aging to older persons in the church. *Dissertation Abstracts International,* December 1972, *33* (6-A), 3011.

Retirement to Florida is tested as a form of "disengagement," both from church attendance and from expression of personal piety. The researcher concludes that age and moving to a new community will speed up the process of disengagement from church involvement and church attendance.

31. Covalt, Nila Kirkpatrick. The meaning of religion to older people—The medical perspective. In Scudder, Delton L. (Ed.), *Organized religion and the older person.* Gainesville: Univ. of Florida Press, 1958, 78-90.

Appealing to her experience as a medical professional, the writer expresses disbelief about people's turning to religion as they grow older, arguing that no one of her patients ever discussed it with her. She does not see people turning to the church for spiritual help when ill.

32. Covalt, Nila Kirkpatrick. The meaning of religion to older people. *Geriatrics,* 1960, *15,* 658-64.

The content of this article is identical with the same writer's paper published two years earlier in Scudder's *Organized Religion and the Older Person* (pp. 78-90). See entry 31.

33. Cowhig, James D., & Schnore, Leo F. Religious affiliation and church attendance in metropolitan centers. *American Catholic Sociological Review,* 1962, *23,* 113-27.

Data obtained through a survey conducted in 1952 in 11 of the largest U.S. cities are used here to analyze factors related to church affiliation and attendance. Six out of 10 Catholics, 2 out of 10 Protestants, and somewhat more than 1 out of 10 Jews reported regular church attendance. While 73% of the Catholics reported attending either regularly or often, less than half the Protestants and only about one-quarter of all Jews reported the same. Table 3 gives a breakdown by age: for those over 60, the figures are 54% Protestants, 76% Catholics, and 33% Jews attending either regularly or often.

34. Dancy, Joseph, Jr. Religiosity and social-psychological adjustment among the Black urban elderly. *Dissertation Abstracts International,* August 1979, *40* (2-A), 1108.

The data for this dissertation were taken from an earlier study on anti-Semitism by Gary T. Marx of the University of California. The total sample for that study consisted of 1,119 Black metropolitan residents, 182 of whom were age 60 and over. The latter group were the respondents in the present dissertation. Among the data were six questions which could serve as measures of "religiosity," and fourteen which could serve as measures of adjustment. Overall, Black elderly showed a higher level of religiosity than others; females, higher than males; those of lower social and economic level proved more religious than those on a higher level in society. It was concluded that "a moderate belief system in which religion is important and God and/or Jesus is significant was more likely to produce happiness than holding strongly to controversial religious beliefs." It was felt that religion was a positive force in helping older urban Blacks of limited income maintain at least a moderate level of adjustment. (University of Michigan, 1978.)

35. Donovan, Harlow. Pastoral needs of older women. *Journal of Pastoral Care,* Fall 1956, *10* (3), 170-76.

The subdivisions of this article are: The Challenge of Later Maturity; Approaching an Understanding of Needs: A Cooperative Method; The Participants (12 Women Aged 80 to 92 Years) and Their Response; An Evaluation of the Project; The Validity of "Felt" Needs; The Hunger for Creative Relationships; Subjective Factors in the Pastoral Relationship; The Existential Question and a Christian Answer.

36. Dowd, J. J., & Lucas, G. Age, religion, and social issues: Evidence from a national sample. *Gerontologist,* 1977, *17* (5, pt. 2), 56.

The writers focus on the differential impact of religious preference on attitudes held throughout the life cycle. The major finding bears on the relative utility of religion as an independent variable in old age and in young adulthood. Religion is called an efficient predictor of attitudes in old age.

37. Edwards, John N., & Klemmack, David L. Correlates of life satisfaction: A re-examination. *Journal of Gerontology,* 1973, *28,* 497-502.

The sample consisted of 507 men and women over the age of 45. The study examines the relationship between life satisfaction and 22 variables, including church-related involvement, which here correlates positively with life satisfaction.

38. Ferguson, Larry N., & Malony, H. Newton. Life satisfaction, the elderly, and organized religious activities. *Gerontologist,* 1975, *15* (5), 69.

A paper presented at the Gerontology Society's scientific meeting in October 1975. It is based on two studies testing the relationship between life satisfaction and participation in organized religion. The setting was a large Southern California church and its "Jolly 60's" department. Church membership did not correlate with life satisfaction, but a significant correlation was found between life satisfaction and the number of activities in which a person participated.

39. Finney, John M., & Lee, Gary R. Age differences on five dimensions of religious involvement. *Review of Religious Research*, 1977, *18* (2), 173-79.

The data came from 493 interviews in Washington state. Seven age cohorts were used, the top two being ages 65-74, and over 74. No numbers are given for any of the cohorts. Age was found to have no effect on five dimensions of religious commitment, except on devotional practice, with which it correlates positively. The investigators suggest that older persons tend to increase devotional activity in an effort to reduce their anxieties. Further research will be required to determine whether the observed relationship is an aging effect or a cohort effect.

40. Frautschi, Barbara. *Local church ministry with older members* (Vol. 1), Program results. *Local church ministry with older members* (Vol. 2), Program methodology. Columbus, Ohio: United Presbyterian Church, 1977.

A study of the older members of 10 local churches in Columbus, 1974 to 1975. The purpose was to determine their needs, to suggest programs and services, and to provide source material on the aging. The second booklet, mimeographed like the first, described the methodology followed, so that the survey could be replicated. Volume 1 contains the results of the survey in Columbus: demographics, church attendance and activities, daily devotions, effect of age on participation in religious activities, appendices containing a bibliography and questionnaires. The reports, pages 4 to 27, are precise and concise. There are 10 tables. Volume 2 on program methodology presents a summary of the program: goals, objectives, and various aspects.

41. Fox, Alfred. How the elderly respond to church. *Christianity Today*, November 20, 1981, *25*, 33.

Sociology professor Alfred Fox was asked to do "roving reporter" interviews among persons at Calvary Church in Santa Ana, California, where he serves as pastor to senior adults. Ten people here give one-paragraph answers to the question, "What is the church doing right and what mistakes is it making in its ministry to older members?"

42. Fukuyama, Yashia. The major dimensions of church membership. *Review of Religious Research*, 1961, *2*, 154-61.

Utilizing Glock's concept of various dimensions in "Religiosity" and analyzing data from 4,000 questionnaires returned from 12 Congregational churches in 7 cities, the writer attempts (among other things) to find the relationship between age and 4 indices of religious orientation. He concludes that there is little difference between young and old on religious formation. On the cultic dimension, there is increased involvement up through age group 50-59, when a decline sets in. The creedal and devotional dimensions show an increase with increasing age.

43. Gitelman, Paul J. Morale, self-concept, and social integration: A comparative study of Black and Jewish aged, urban poor. *Dissertation Abstracts International,* Dec. 1976, *37* (6-A), 3907-08.

This study finds that religion, race, and ethnicity have an impact on adjustment to old age. The hypothesized strength of the married Jewish female is not confirmed. The profound actual and potential impact of religion on the respondents is stressed.

44. Glock, Charles Y. On the study of religious commitment. *Religious Education,* July-Aug. 1962, *57* (suppl.), 98-110.

Although this article does not specifically consider the aged in their relation to what has been called "religiosity," it is nevertheless included in this bibliography because of its importance in defining the concept "religion" as used in many of the studies that do concern religion and aging. Glock discusses what might be required for a useful definition of religion and suggests a strategy for meeting these requirements. Five "dimensions of religiosity" are proposed: the experiential, the ritualistic, the ideological, the intellectual, and the consequential. No single piece of research, he feels, has looked at all five.

45. Glock, Charles Y.; Ringer, Benjamin B.; & Babbie, Earl R. *To comfort and to challenge: A dilemma of the contemporary church.* Los Angeles: Univ. of California Press, 1967.

Research done for the Protestant Episcopal church, to determine the strength of the members' ties to their church—why some are more deeply involved than others, and what difference this involvement makes. Though this study is not exclusively about the elderly, it does include them in its various aspects.

46. Gray, Robert M. The personal adjustment of the older person in the church. In Vedder, Clyde B. (Ed.), *Gerontology: A book of readings.* Springfield, Ill.: Charles C. Thomas, 1963, 336-42.

This is a revised version of a paper read at a joint meeting of the American Sociological Society and the Society for the Study of Social Problems in 1955. As such, it was published in *Sociology and Social Research,* Jan. 1957, *1,* 175-80. The material is from the author's doctoral dissertation at the University of Chicago in 1954. The aged members of two Chicago area church groups were studied to determine the role of their church experience with regard to their personal adjustment. Nearly all older church members had good or average personal adjustment, but no significant differences were found between young and old.

47. Gray, Robert M., & Moberg, David O. *The church and the older person* (Rev. ed.). Grand Rapids: Wm. B. Eerdmans Co., 1977.

This is a revision of a work originally published in 1962, with the findings of social research on the place of religion in the lives of older people, their problems, their religion, their personal adjustment; what the church can do for them, and what they can do for the church.

48. Growing old gracefully in St. Louis. *America*, 28 January 1956, *94*, 468-69.

This unsigned editorial comments on a special study of the elderly members in a St. Louis Catholic parish [St. Philip Neri]. Interviewed were 437 persons, 60 years of age or older. Four-fifths of them still attended weekly Mass; three-fourths still came to church each month for confession; more than half received communion weekly. Most of them wanted to be self-supporting as long as they could; and in fact, three-fourths of them still relied on their own means for daily living expenses.

49. Heenan, Edward F. Sociology of religion and the aged: The empirical lacunae. *Journal for the Scientific Study of Religion*, 1972, *11* (2), 171-76.

Despite the opening sentence of the printed summary on page 171, this article is not "a comprehensive bibliography on the relation between religion and aging." It is a very good survey of the *sociological* literature, "a survey of 140 social science journals," with a critical evaluation of what has been written about religion and aging from that particular standpoint. The writer finds that there have been four major areas of research: (a) church attendance, (b) religion and the personal adjustment of the elderly, (c) the meaning of religion to the elderly, and (d) religion and death. Sociologists, he notes, have contributed very little to the study of religion and aging.

50. Ingraham, M. H., & Mulanaphy, J. M. *My purpose holds: Reactions and experiences in retirement of TIAA-CREF annuitants.* New York: Teachers' Insurance and Annuity Association, n.d.

The reactions and experiences of these retirees include some of their opinions about religion and churches vis-a-vis the elderly.

51. Jacobs, Ruth H. The sabbath is for rest. *Long Term Care and Health Services Administration*, 1978, *2* (1), 20-28.

Jacobs, a sociologist, studied the way in which being able to work, or being unable to do so, after age 65 affected older persons' spiritual and religious lives. Of 4 cases, the 3 people who were able to work after 65 at new and different jobs seemed well adjusted; the fourth, who was unable to work, was depressed and suicidal. The writer concludes that "a value system that puts a premium on work makes it hard for many unemployed senior citizens (she actually studied 90) to feel at ease."

52. Jeffers, Frances C., & Nichols, Claude R.   The relationship of activities and attitudes to physical well-being in older people. *Journal of Gerontology*, 1961, *16*, 67-70.

The Duke University Medical Center tested 251 volunteers on the abovementioned relationship. The Activity Inventory of Cavan, Burgess, Havighurst, and Goldhamer was used; all categories of the activity scale were significantly related to physical functioning, with the exception of religious activity. On the attitude scale, an inverse relationship was found between physical functioning and religion. As the end of life was approaching, religion meant more to the subjects, especially older disabled persons, who were more highly motivated to religion.

53. Johnson, Arthur L.; Brekke, Milo L.; Strommen, Merton; & Underwager, Ralph C.   Age differences and dimensions of religious behavior. *Journal of Social Issues*, 1974, *30* (3), 43-67.

This research was done on a national sample of 4,444 Lutheran church members, ages 15-65, to explore the magnitude, sources, and consequences of differences among age groups of various dimensions of religious orientation and practice. The oldest of the 6 age groups considered was 50-65.

54. Johnson, Lois Mary.   Religious patterns, coping mechanisms, and life satisfaction of the Black and White aged. *Dissertation Abstracts International*, April 1979, *39* (10-A), 6337.

An exploratory study of the religious patterns manifested by aged Blacks and Whites to determine whether this religious involvement increased their life satisfaction by enabling them to cope with aging. The major hypotheses were confirmed: (a) Black aged manifested greater religiosity than White aged, (b) Black made greater use of religion as a coping mechanism, (c) both Black and White aged attain similar levels of life satisfaction.

55. Johnson, Marilyn E.   Religious roles. In Riley, Matilda White, & Foner, Anne (Eds.), *Aging and society* (Vol. 1). New York: Russell Sage Foundation, 1968, 483-500.

Data are offered concerning religious identification, church attendance, religious association, beliefs, importance of religion, religion and life satisfaction.

56. Kivett, Vira R.   Religious motivation in middle age: Correlates and implications. *Journal of Gerontology*, 1979, *34* (1), 106-15.

Although the age range of the men and women studied is only 45-65, "the findings suggest that an important relationship may exist between the 'comfort' and the 'challenge' functions of religion and spiritual well-being in later life for middle-aged groups."

57. Kuhlen, Raymond G. Trends in religious behavior during the adult years. In Little, Lawrence C. (Ed.), *Wider horizons in Christian adult education.* Pittsburgh: Univ. of Pittsburgh Press, 1962, 1-26.

Summarizes some of the available findings in the psychology of religion. Deals with the problem of defining "religion," of overt vs. covert behavior, of living "the good life." The cultural context of research; secular trends and subcultural contrasts. The psychological correlates of religiousness. Tables on the changes in reasons for attending church by age groups (the oldest of which is "50 plus"); religious practices of Catholics in Southern City (oldest group, "60 plus"); church attendance (oldest, "65 plus"). The table on page 21 regarding the changes in religious attitudes and activities in late maturity (60 to beyond 90) is taken from Ruth Cavan et al., *Personal Adjustment in Old Age* (Chicago, 1949).

58. Kurlychek, Robert T. Level of the belief in afterlife and four categories of fear and death in a sample of 60+ year olds. *Psychological Reports,* 1976, *38,* 228.

The purpose of this study was to investigate the relationship between belief in an afterlife and 4 categories of "fear of death." The sample included only 10 males and 30 females, ranging in age from 60 to 82 years. The only significant correlation was found between belief in afterlife and "fear of death of others." There was no significant correlation between believing in afterlife and the other 3 categories, "fear of death of self," "fear of dying of self," and "fear of dying of others."

59. Larue, Gerald A. Religion and the aged. In Burnside, Irene M. (Ed.), *Nursing and the aged.* New York: McGraw-Hill Book Co., 1976, 573-83.

How religious beliefs may affect and determine attitudes of personal identity and worth, thereby influencing the way an individual thinks and feels about aging. Emphasizes potentials, explores innate qualities of being human, discusses aging and death.

60. Lawton, M. Powell; Kleban, Morton H.; & Singer, Maurice. The aged Jewish person and the slum environment. *Journal of Gerontology,* 1971, *26,* 231-39.

Interviews with elderly Jewish slum residents in order to learn of their needs and how they compared with the elderly in general. Those interviewed fell below the standards of the general population on all counts, including religious attendance.

61. Lazerwitz, Bernard. Some factors associated with variations in church attendance. *Social Forces,* 1961, *39,* 301-09.

Church attendance, as reported by three survey research centers, is analyzed in various ways, with conclusions reported according to sex, race, religion, etc. Analysis of the age factor shows no change in church attendance as a person ages. Table 3 on page 304 gives the frequency of church attendance by age (highest category, "65 and over") for various faiths.

62. Lebowitz, Barry P.   Age and religiosity in an urban ethnic community. *Gerontologist*, 1973, *13* (3, pt. 2), 65.

Conclusions drawn about generational differences in religiosity among Jewish Americans, so this author claims, have been based on measures possessing doubtful validity. Typically, measurement has been confined to ritual participation or congregational membership. This study conceptualizes religion as a multi-dimensional phenomenon. Interviews with a representative sample of 312 Portland, Oregon, household heads strongly confirm the multi-dimensional hypothesis. Age was a significant cleavage: relatively few issues were touched on which the different age groups were in agreement.

63. Lepkowski, J. Richard.   The attitudes and adjustments of institutionalized and non-institutionalized Catholic aged. *Journal of Gerontology*, 1956, *11*, 185-91.

The 93 institutionalized individuals of this study, aged 65 to 95, were all from one home in New York City. The 32 noninstitutionalized individuals, 60 to 84 years old, were all members of one club. No significant differences were found between the 2 groups, nor even between matched pairs, when scored on their attitudes or their levels of adjustment. Religion was among attitudes sampled.

64. McDowell, John.   Religious needs of older Americans. In Cull, John G., & Hardy, Richard E. (Eds.), *The neglected older American. Social and rehabilitation service.* Springfield, Ill.: Charles C. Thomas, 1973, 110-17.

Religion is here described as "the response to all of life" and "the search for meaning in the range of life's experiences." Religious needs are then seen in coping with loneliness, a need for companionship, guilt feelings, and facing death. There is a section on chaplaincies in institutions caring for the aged.

65. McIsaac, Sister Mary Trinita.   The spirituality of the older Sister. *Review for Religious*, March 1973, *32*, 295-97.

The author's purpose is not to suggest a program of spiritual exercises or prayer forms but to understand the prevailing situation and its underlying causes. Elderly Sisters may experience insecurity and tensions with respect to their faith because of changes in cultural base, in life style, and in theology of holiness. They can be expected to give evidence of meditation and faith, of the serenity and dignity of those who have integrated the meaning of life and death into the whole of human existence.

66. Marshall, Helen, & Odom, Melita.   The status of the mature gifted individual as a basis for evaluation of the aging process. *Gerontologist*, 1962, *2*, 201-06.

(Citation 66 continued)

The Terman Gifted Group. The sample size at this time (1962) was about 1,500. Questionnaires of the years 1950 and 1960 were compared, and a slight trend was noted toward increased interest in religion, especially on the part of the women, 40% of whom listed religious activities in 1950, compared with 60% in 1960. About 58% of the men and 68% of the women were members of some church or religiously oriented group.

67. Martin, David, & Wrightsman, Lawrence S., Jr. Religion and fears about death: A critical review of research. *Religious Education*, 1964, 59, 174-76.

Much of the meager research dealing with religion and fears about death, these writers think, may be criticized with regard to the measures used, the samples studied, and the generalizations made from the findings. The purpose of their paper is to make suggestions for new directions which might be taken.

68. Martin, David, & Wrightsman, Lawrence S., Jr. The relationship between religious behavior and concern about death. *Journal of Social Psychology*, 1965, 65, 317-23.

Fifty-eight adults of three Protestant congregations were surveyed concerning religious attitudes, religious participation, and fear of death. Older members, and those reporting more religious participation, showed less fear of death than others.

69. Mindel, Charles H., & Vaughan, C. Edwin. A multidimensional approach to religiosity and disengagement. *Journal of Gerontology*, 1978, 33, 103-08.

This study of 106 elderly Missourians examines religious behavior as a form of disengagement. It is argued that religiosity must be measured in both its organizational forms (such as attending religious services) and also in its more subjective nonorganizational forms. Data support the thesis that the elderly may be disengaged organizationally and still be engaged nonorganizationally.

70. Moberg, David Oscar. Religion and personal adjustment in old age. A study of some aspects of the Christian religion in relation to personal adjustment of the aged in institutions. *Dissertation Abstracts*, 1952, 12, 341-42.

The author studied the personal adjustment of 219 persons aged 65 and over, residents of seven institutions in the Twin City area. Church membership in and of itself appeared unrelated to personal adjustment in old age, but better-adjusted people were more active religiously, and religious "believers" were better adjusted in old age than "nonbelievers." (Citations 70-75 refer to this same study.)

71. Moberg, David O. Leadership in the church and personal adjustment in old age. *Sociology and Social Research*, 1953, *37*, 312-16.

Persons in this study sample who had once been leaders in the church were found to be better adjusted in old age, as a group, than others who had never held positions of leadership. It is possible that there was some causal relationship between church leadership and personal adjustment. It is also possible that some third factor was the cause of this good personal adjustment in old age and of leadership in the church. (See citation 70.)

72. Moberg, David O. Church membership and personal adjustment in old age. *Journal of Gerontology*, 1953, 8, 207-11.

In this study, questionnaires were completed by 219 persons living in seven institutions of the Minneapolis-St. Paul area. Personal adjustment in old age was measured by the Burgess-Cavan-Havighurst Attitudes Inventory. For 132 church members, the mean adjustment score was 28.4, while it was only 23.3 for 86 nonmembers. This difference was significant at the .01 level of confidence. Matching individuals from each group on the basis of 7 control factors reduced the score of members to 26.8, and raised that of nonmembers to 24.9 – a difference not significant even at the .05 level. Adding 2 more control factors reduced the sample to 18 persons, 9 in each group; now, the nonmembers came out slightly ahead. (See citation 70.)

73. Moberg, David O. The Christian religion and personal adjustment in old age. *American Sociological Review*, 1953, *18*, 87-90.

This paper summarizes the chief findings of a 1951 study of 219 persons aged 65 and over, residents of seven institutions in the Twin City metropolitan area. (See citation 70.) For the sample of persons studied, good personal adjustment was probably due to religious activities and beliefs associated with church membership, rather than due to church affiliation as such. Former church leaders were better adjusted in old age than other members.

74. Moberg, David O. Religion and personal adjustment in old age: A study of some aspects of the Christian religion in relation to personal adjustment of the aged in institutions. *Religious Education*, May-June 1953, *48*, 184-85.

A summary description of Moberg's 1952 Ph.D. dissertation at the University of Minnesota. The 219 subjects of the study, aged 65 and over, were residents of 5 homes for the aged and 2 similar institutions. It was concluded that religion is one of the many important factors related to personal adjustment in old age. (See citation 70.)

75. Moberg, David O. Religious activities and personal adjustment in old age. *Journal of Social Psychology*, 1956, *43*, 261-67.

The study reported here is part of the larger study made in 1951. (See citation 70.) The subjects were 219 persons, aged 65 and older, living in seven institutions of the Minneapolis-St. Paul area. A significant correlation ($r = .59$) was found between personal adjustment in old age and a religious activities score based on past and present religious experience. Either those who are well adjusted engage in many religious activities, or engaging in many religious activities contributes to good personal adjustment in old age.

76. Moberg, David O.   Christian beliefs and personal adjustment to old age. *American Scientific Affiliation Journal*, 1958, *10*, 8-12.

Moberg's hypothesis was "that the tendency of many old people to cling to or to return to religious faith is related to good personal adjustment in old age." In a sample of 68 elderly persons, he matched 51 "fundamentalist" church members with 7 "nonfundamentalists" on the basis of 11 characteristics. Matched control and experimental groups of 6 persons each showed greater differences in mean personal adjustment scores than those that prevailed between the unmatched groups, "fundamentalists" in both cases having higher mean personal adjustment scores. The differences, however, were not statistically significant. The writer concludes that, for the samples that have been studied, the holding of orthodox or conservative Christian beliefs is related to good personal adjustment in old age.

77. Moberg, David O.   Religion in old age. *Geriatrics*, 1965, *20*, 977-82.

There are two reasons why researchers have reached contradictory conclusions about the role of religion in aging: (a) the personal bias of the researcher, and (b) different concepts of religion. Moberg here repeats Glock's five dimensions of religiosity (see Glock, 1962, in this same section of our bibliography) and adds a sixth "spiritual" one of his own. Physicians need to appreciate the importance of religion in health care and in therapy.

78. Moberg, David O.   Religiosity in old age. *Gerontologist*, 1965, *5* (2), 78-87.

Contradictory answers to questions about religion in later life are due to differences in defining "religion" and "religiosity," as well as to personal bias of the investigators. After briefly explaining Glock's five "dimensions of religiosity," Moberg summarizes the research findings for each dimension. Having thus surveyed the studies done to date, he suggests that ritualistic behavior outside the home tends to diminish with increasing age, while religious attitudes and feelings seem to increase among people who have an acknowledged religion. (See also citation 77.)

79. Moberg, David O.   Religion and the aging family. *Family Coordinator*, January 1972, *21* (1), 47-60. [Reprinted in *Lutheran Social Concern*, Summer 1972, *12* (2), 9-27.]

"Although extra-domicilial religious practices tend to decrease during the later years, internalized religious attitudes and feelings apparently increase.

(Citation 79 continued)
. . . Churches can contribute to family integration, the changing of societal values, the satisfaction of needs, and opportunities for meaningful service; but their activities sometimes have dysfunctional consequences also." The bibliography on pages 58-60 is extensive, but is not limited to the religious aspects of aging.

80. Moberg, David O.   Spiritual well-being in late life. In Gubrium, Jaber F. (Ed.), *Late life: Communities and environmental policy*. Springfield, Ill.: Charles C. Thomas, 1974, 256-79.

On the nature of spiritual needs in late life and various points relevant to research on this subject. Subdivisions of the chapter are: What Is Spiritual Well-Being? ("The inner resources of people, their ultimate concern around which all other values are focused, their central philosophy of life"); Spiritual Needs in Late Life; Channels to Satisfy Spiritual Needs; Scientific Analysis of Spiritual Well-Being; Research Findings; Indicators of Spiritual Well-Being; Consequences of Spiritual Well-Being.

81. Moberg, David O., & Taves, Marvin J.   Church participation and adjustment in old age. In Rose, A. M., & Peterson, W. A. (Eds.), *Older people and their social world*. Philadelphia: F. A. Davis, 1965, 113-24.

The purpose of this study was to analyze data from a broad, community-based sample and test the hypothesis that church participation during old age is correlated with good personal adjustment. Based on interviews with 5,000 persons aged 60 and over, from four midwestern states. Adjustment was measured by the Burgess-Cavan-Havighurst Attitudes Inventory. The hypothesis was confirmed.

82. The myth and reality of aging in America.   Washington, D.C.: National Council on the Aging, 1975.

A study done for the National Council on the Aging by Lou Harris and Associates, Inc., in April, 1975. Questions on religion are to be found on pages 180-82. Tables on: Importance of Religion in Your Life, Attendance at a Church or Synagogue in the Last Year or So, and Religion of the Public.

83. Nelson, Franklyn L.   Religiosity and self-destructive crises in the institutionalized elderly. *Suicide and Life-Threatening Behavior*, 1977, 7 (2), 67-74.

A rating scale, devised to measure indirect life-threatening behavior, was administered to 58 patients in a VA hospital. Findings indicated that "intensity of religious commitment is a potentially more meaningful measure of religiosity than is formal church membership"; and that "intensity of religious commitment varies inversely with the extent of indirect self-destructive activity."

84. Nugent, Frank McGill. The disengagement theory of aging and retirement applied to clergymen. *Dissertation Abstracts International,* April 1976, *36* (10-A), 5358.

The subjects were 150 clergymen between ages 65 and 75 representing 3 distinct life styles: a married clergy, unmarried priests belonging to a diocese, and unmarried priests who were members of a religious community. The sample also represented the work roles of the pastoral minister and the educator/administrator. In some instances the disengagement theory was supported by the data; in others, it was not. Clergymen remained engaged in their work beyond retirement age to a significantly higher degree than men of other callings. The data rather favored the activity theory; those who had a high engagement index showed a higher degree of life satisfaction.

85. Orbach, Harold L. Aging and religion: A study of church attendance in the Detroit metropolitan area. *Geriatrics,* 1961, *16,* 530-40.

The population consisted of 6,911 adults aged 21 and over in the Detroit metropolitan area. Church attendance in this group failed to confirm the hypothesis that religious behavior would increase among the elderly. It is suggested that the religious observance of older people depends on other factors than age.

86. O'Reilly, Charles T. Religious practice and personal adjustment of older people. *Sociology and Social Research,* Nov.-Dec. 1957, *42,* 119-21. Reprinted in Vedder, Clyde B. (Ed.), *Gerontology: A book of readings.* Springfield, Ill.: Charles C. Thomas, 1963, 343-46.

Two hundred ten Catholics over 65 in a working-class Chicago community were questioned about their religious practice and personal adjustment. Women were more "active" than men, and religious activity tended to increase as people got older. Of those under 75, 45.5% were "active" in practicing their religion, as compared with 67.4% of those over 75. When asked whether their religion had become more helpful to them in the last 10 years, 49% felt that it had. Older people who were lonely or unhappy did not turn to religion more than other older people did.

87. O'Rourke, William D. The relationship between religiousness, purpose-in-life, and fear of death. *Dissertation Abstracts International,* May 1977, *37* (11-A), 7046-47.

This study was designed to examine the relationship between religious commitment, purpose-in-life, and fear of death in a sample of elderly nursing home residents, male and female, aged 65 to 96, with a median of 80 years. Religiousness was assessed only by measuring the ideological or belief dimension; purpose in life was established by the test of Crumbaugh and Maholick; fear of death was measured on a scale devised by Donald

Templar. The hypothesis, that religiousness and higher purpose in life would be related, was supported by the data. No relationship was found between religiousness and fear of death.

88. Palmore, Erdman B.   The effects of aging on activities and attitudes. *Gerontologist*, 1968, 8, 259-63.

A longitudinal study, consisting of four rounds of interviews between 1955 and 1967, used the Burgess-Cavan-Havighurst-Goldhamer Activity and Attitude Inventory on 127 subjects. Religious attitude scores were found to have no correlation with total attitude; at any given point, religious items could be dropped or considered separately without affecting the results.

89. Pan, Ju-Shu.   Personal adjustments of old people: A study of old people in Protestant church homes for the aged. *Sociology and Social Research*, Sept.-Oct. 1950, 35, 3-11.

A study of 730 old people selected from homes for the aged sponsored by Protestant religious groups in northern U.S.A. Findings were compared with those of a similar study which Ruth Cavan had done of 499 males and 759 females, most of whom were living in their own homes. Participation in religious activities is reported on pages 10-11; it was found that the institutionalized elderly attended religious services more frequently than they had earlier in life. Half of these subjects were from the Methodist church. (See citations 90-92.)

90. Pan, Ju-Shu.   Factors in the personal adjustment of old people in Protestant homes for the aged. *American Sociological Review*, 1951, 16, 379-81.

This study attempted to measure the influence of institutionalization on personal adjustment of 730 men and women in old age. (See citations 89-92.)

91. Pan, Ju-Shu.   A comparison of factors in the personal adjustment of old people in the Protestant church homes for the aged, and old people living outside of institutions. *Journal of Social Psychology*, 1952, 35, 195-203.

The purpose of this study was to examine the influence of institutionalization on personal adjustment in old age. The subjects were 597 institutionalized women, 65 years of age and over, living in 68 Protestant church homes, who were then compared with the 759 elderly women who had been studied by Mrs. Cavan. Findings, though tentative, suggested that the aged living in their own homes were better adjusted. Participation in religious activities was higher in the institution than among those living outside; the exact data are given in a table on page 201. (See citation 92.)

92. Pan, Ju-Shu.   Institutional and personal adjustment in old age. *Journal of Genetic Psychology*, 1954, 85, 155-58.

The influence of institutionalization on personal adjustment of 597 women in old age. (See citation 91.)

93. Payne, Barbara Pittard. Religious life of the elderly: Myth or reality? In Thorson, James A., & Cook, Thomas C., Jr. (Eds.), *Spiritual well-being of the elderly*. Springfield, Ill.: Charles C. Thomas, 1980, 218-29.

The writer feels it is generally assumed that religion becomes increasingly important to older people as they near death. Research to support this assumption has been limited, and results have been contradictory. Most information is based on empirical studies which are from 10 to 25 years old; their measures, methodology, and their very concept of "religion" make generalizations hazardous. Major books on aging have devoted but little space to the religious aspect. After surveying the literature thus criticized, the writer makes some recommendations.

94. Query, Joy M., & Steines, Meriel. Disillusionment, health status, and age: A study of value differences of midwestern women. *International Journal of Aging and Human Development*, Summer 1974, 5 (3), 245-56.

In a midwestern metropolitan community, 148 young, middle-aged, and older women were tested for disillusionment with major American values. It was found that religious optimism decreased with age.

95. Reboul, Hélène. Vieillard et l'après-mort. *Archives de Sciences Sociales des Religions*, Jan.-June 1975, 20, 169-74.

"Notes sur l'état d'une recherche." A number of interviews were held with the elderly about the death of other people, about keeping the memory of the dead, and about one's own death. A vocabulary analysis was done on these interviews. Attention was focused on images associated with the body at the moment of death and afterwards. It was thought that this methodological study should lead to a better understanding of old age, as well as to a perspective on death in our Western society.

96. Reid, W. S.; Gilmore, Anne J. J.; Andrews, G. R.; & Caird, F. I. A study of religious attitudes of the elderly. *Age and Ageing*, 1978, 7, 40-45.

"The elderly" in this study were 501 people aged 65 and over, randomly selected from among those living at home, in the west of Scotland. Included were 181 men and 320 women, of whom 79 and 153 respectively were aged 75 or more. The questionnaire administered included data on religious upbringing, church attendance, religious beliefs, and involvement in church activities. Six tables record denomination, church attendance, comfort from religion, comfort in bereavement, belief in after-life, and fear of death. Percentages are given for men and for women, for Protestant and Catholic, for church affiliation and nonaffiliation. The conclusion is that religious beliefs and activities, which make explicit reference to a supernatural source of values, remain important to the majority of the present elderly population of Scotland. Questions on religious attitudes are produced in an appendix.

97. Rogers, Tommy. Manifestations of religiosity and the aging process. *Religious Education*, July-August 1976, *71*, 405-15.

Section 1 is on the gerontological functions of religion; namely, to face impending death, to give meaning to life, to help accept the losses of old age, to discover compensatory values, to meet secular and social needs. Section 2 is devoted to the "religiosity of the aged." Several hypotheses are advanced to account for a tendency to become more religious with advancing age; these are: diminished life space and opportunity, egocentric defense, decreased mental capacity, increased tendency to introspection, putative and punitive control, etc. Summary on pages 414-15.

98. Shulik, Richard Norman. Faith development, moral development, and old age: an assessment of Fowler's faith development paradigm. *Dissertation Abstracts International*, December 1979, *40* (6-B), 2907.

In a research design involving forty subjects (20 men and 20 women) between the ages of 56 and 86, it was found that the faith-development stage is significantly related to the respondent's subjective awareness of the changes taking place in old age. Contrary to Butler and Erikson, almost none of the subjects were engaging in a life review, and almost none were preparing for death. (University of Chicago, 1979.)

99. Siegel, Martha Kaufer. A Jewish aging experience: A description of the role of religion in response to physical dysfunction in a sample of Jewish women 65 to 83. *Dissertation Abstracts International*, August 1977, *38* (2-A), 722.

Explores the variation in the experience of physical aging among a group of 33 women, aged 65 to 83, living within the Jewish subculture. A distinctly Jewish response to the aging process is described as being generally positive. For the study group, religion provided an avenue for compensatory values and a viable female role in advanced age; however, their religion did not provide comfort by resolving health-related belief dilemmas. Orientation toward religion is specified as "world view" in the hierarchical system of faith stages, according to James Fowler.

100. Singh, Kripal. Religiosity among the aged. *Indian Journal of Gerontology*, 1970, *2*, 71-73.

Religious orientation was studied in 390 subjects, aged 55 and over, belonging to various religious communities of Lucknow City. On the basis of his questionnaire, the author concludes that "early realization of the role of religion results in a decrease of religious faith (with age), whereas late realization results in an increase in religious faith with age."

101. Spreitzer, Elmer, & Snyder, Eldon E. Correlates of life satisfaction among the aged. *Journal of Gerontology*, 1974, *29*, 454-58.

Church attendance correlates .08 with life satisfaction, in contrast to a high of .24 correlation of financial security with life satisfaction and of .25 for "self-assessed health." The church attendance correlation is the lowest positive one to be found in the table on page 455; it is lower than any of the variables in the socioeconomic or social psychological categories. Within its own category of "background characteristics," it ranks lower than race (.12) and marital status (.09).

102. Stafford, Virginia. Role of the church in education for aging. *Adult Leadership, 1960, 9* (1), 16-33.

In the educational planning of the churches, the needs of older people play a large role today. This article presents a tentative list of so-called spiritual needs of the aging: Assurance of God's Continuing Love, The Certainty That Life Is Protected, Relief from Heightened Emotions, Relief from the Pangs of Loneliness, A Perspective That Embraces Time and Eternity, Continuing Spiritual Growth, A Satisfying Status in Life, A Feeling of Continuing Usefulness.

103. Stark, Rodney. Age and faith: A changing outlook on an old process. *Sociological Analysis, 1968, 29* (1), 1-10.

It is often said that personal religious commitment increases with age, partly because of a fear of death. It is also said that the apparent increase in piety among the aged is not due to age but to cohort effect. This study reports evidence for both sides, depending on the aspect of religious commitment that is examined.

104. Steinitz, Lucy Y. Religion, well-being, and Weltanschauung: Preliminary perspectives. *Gerontologist,* Oct. 1978, *18* (5, pt. 2), 129. Also in *Journal for the Scientific Study of Religion,* March 1980, *19* (1), 60-67.

Four measures of religiosity (drawn from the NORC General Social Survey) were examined to determine how well they predicted 13 self-reported questions on personal well-being, life satisfaction, and the world view of elderly persons. Only the measure "frequency of church attendance" resulted in consistent associations with well-being, especially among older women. Belief in life after death was shown to be a much stronger and more discriminating predictor, both of well-being and of *Weltanschauung.* Age was a better predictor of both dependent variables than were any of the religious measures. Older people were found to be more religious than were people under 65 (out of the total sample size of 9,120, there were 1,493 subjects who were 65 and older). However, contrary to some earlier findings, older people who are religious do not have consistently greater feelings of well-being, nor a better *Weltanschauung,* than older people who are less religious.

105. Stone, Jane Livermore, & Norris, Arthur H. Activities and attitudes of participants in the Baltimore Longitudinal Study. *Journal of Gerontology, 1966, 21,* 575-80.

(Citation 105 continued)

Activity and attitude inventories of Burgess-Cavan-Havighurst-Gold-hamer were administered to 463 male participants in the above-mentioned study. Of these, 151 were beyond the age of 60. The longitudinal study was to compare young and old; no significant trends were found.

106. Swenson, Wendell M.   Attitudes toward death in an aging popula-tion. *Journal of Gerontology*, 1961, *16*, 49-52.

Death attitudes of 210 persons over 60 years of age, all residents of Min-nesota. Two separate methods were used to evaluate their attitudes: a checklist and written essays. A significant relationship was found between religiosity and attitudes toward death. Persons with more fundamental religious convictions looked forward to death more than others; fearful at-titudes tended to be found in persons with little religious activity.

107. Theisen, Sylvester.   A social survey of aged Catholics in the deanery of Fort Wayne, Indiana.   *Dissertation Abstracts*, June 1962, *22* (12, pt. 1), 4434-35.

The impact of aging upon the sociocultural and economic status of a ran-dom sample of 506 Catholics aged 65 and over. The interview schedule in-cluded 79 questions, a few of them about religion and views of life. Increas-ing age brought a decrease in church attendance, frequently because of ill health or low economic status.

108. Therese, Sister Mary.   *A study of aging in a Cleveland parish.* Washington, D.C.: National Conference of Catholic Charities, 1954, 1-72.

The study of 320 aging persons in a Cleveland parish: to explore their needs, to share information obtained from them, to interest others in help-ing them. There is a summary on page 21, followed by more than 50 pages of questionnaires and data, with 33 tables.

109. Thorson, James A., & Cook, Thomas C., Jr. (Eds.).   *Spiritual well-being of the elderly.* Springfield, Ill.: Charles C. Thomas, 1980.

From the dust jacket: "This pioneering book argues that spiritual well-being is an important element in the quality of life of older adults that has been overlooked by gerontologists. Thirty chapters by persons from diverse disciplines related to both gerontology and theology provide a broad perspective of research and practical applications in this field. . . . Spiritual Well-Being of the Elderly maps out the common ground between geron-tology, theology, and philosophy."

110. Waterman, Leroy.   Religion and religious observance in old age. In Tibbits, Clark, & Donahue, Wilma (Eds.), *Aging in today's society.* Englewood Cliffs: Prentice Hall, 1960, 307-15.

The aging need a feeling of security that comes from activities that are heartwarming and worthwhile. Wise old men and women can help us solve society's problems.

111. Williams, Robert L., & Cole, Spurgeon. Religiosity, generalized anxiety, and apprehension concerning death. *Journal of Social Psychology,* 1968, *78*, 111-17.

These researchers tested Freud's hypothesis that religion is the product of insecurity. There should then be a negative correlation between religiousness and security. But when three degrees of religiosity were matched with three types of anxiety, it was found that the highly religious subjects manifested the least insecurity on all dimensions, while the low religion group had the greatest generalized insecurity.

112. Wingrove, C. Ray, & Alston, Jon P. Age, aging, and church attendance. *Gerontologist,* 1971, *11* (pt. 1), 356-58.

The literature dealing with age, aging, and church attendance reports contradictory findings, depending on whether the studies used cross-sectional or retrospective data. Longitudinal data from the period 1939-69, using cohort analysis, suggests that church attendance trends are very sensitive to changes in the social environment, regardless of age or sex or cohort.

113. Wittkowski, J., & Baumgartner, I. Religiosität und Einstellung zu Tod und Sterben bei alten Menschen. (Religiosity and attitude towards death and dying in elderly persons.) *Zeitschrift für Gerontologie,* Jan.-Feb. 1977, *10* (1), 61-68.

Attitudes towards death and dying held by 60 residents of homes for the aged. These attitudes are analyzed in relation to six dimensions of religiousness. A high correlation is found between deep religiosity and a positive, anxiety-free attitude towards death.

114. Wygant, W. E. Why me, Lord? *Pastoral Psychology,* October 1972, *23*, 29-36.

Extra years of life often present a challenge to the elderly individual and to those involved in his care. The challenge for terminal geriatric patients in particular could be worded, "How can I maintain my sense of personal worth, my sense of selfhood and value to others, to the very end?" Maslow's five levels of human need. Most of this article is a detailed case history illustrating a patient's anger and providing an account of the author's counseling sessions with him.

II. ORGANIZED RELIGION IN THE SERVICE OF THE ELDERLY

115. Abraams, Edith. Religion in the rehabilitation of the aged. In Thorson, James A., & Cook, Thomas C., Jr. (Eds.), *Spiritual well-being of the elderly*. Springfield, Ill.: Charles C. Thomas, 1980, 187-94.

This report describes an experiment at the Hebrew Rehabilitation Center for the Aged in Boston, carried out over a period of a year and a half, on a forty-bed unit housing the most physically and mentally deteriorated men, 80 to 100 years old. The point was not to impose religious practices, but to awaken memories of ceremonies from earlier days. "A number of the patients developed more stature in their own eyes and in the reflection of those around them."

116. Affiliated Lutheran social service agencies and institutions. Minneapolis: Lutheran Social Service System, 1979.

A directory of Lutheran-affiliated hospitals, institutions, and social service agencies, some of which (like homes for the aged) serve the elderly either principally or exclusively. Refer to the Lutheran Social Service System, 2414 Park Avenue, Minneapolis MN 55404, tel. 612/871-0227.

117. The Aged: A Symposium. *New Catholic World*, May-June 1980, *223*, 100-34.

Contributions to this symposium were the following: "The Problem of Dependence" by Drew Christiansen; "Challenge of Aging in the Church" by Victorina Peralta; "The Parish Includes the Elderly" by Edward Gorry; "The New Realities of Retirement" by Barry Robinson; "Ethical Issues on Aging and Dying" by Andrew Varga; "Gray Panthers Focus on Aging" by Kathleen Connolly; "Center for the Study of Retirement" by Dismas McAuliffe; "The Elderly in the Parish Community" by Charles Fahey; "Serving the Needs of the Spirit" by Virginia Sloyan; "Keen Agers" by Wilbert Standenmaier.

118. Aging—the challenge to the church. *Lutheran Social Concern*, Summer 1972, *12* (2), 8.

This periodical, *Lutheran Social Concern*, was formerly known as *Lutheran Social Welfare*. Volume 12, number 2, was a special issue on aging, meant to challenge the church in its ministry and to challenge aging persons to recognize their responsibility as well. Articles include: "Religion and the Aging Family," "The Aging: Outreach Services Provided by Congregation and Community," "Service Programs for the Aged through Social Institutions," "The Rights of Older Persons," and "Perspective."

119. Ailor, James W. The church provides for the elderly. In Boyd, Rosamonde Ramsay, & Oakes, Charles G. (Eds.), *Foundations of practical gerontology* (2d ed.). Columbia: Univ. of South Carolina Press, 1973, 205-20.

(Citation 119 continued)
The church must give people a renewed sense of selfhood, dignity, creativity, and purpose for living. The writer sees the church's role in providing services for the elderly basically in these categories: (a) ministry to the homebound, (b) ministry to the sick and dying, (c) counseling services to three-generational families, (d) providing a program that stimulates the creativity of people who feel that their day is past, (e) providing housing and supportive service. There is also a description of the "XYZ" (Extra Years of Zest) group in the writer's own Methodist church in Louisiana.

120. American Lutheran Church. *To stand alongside.* Minneapolis: American Lutheran Church, 1970.

Seven chapters and a state-by-state directory of agencies certified by the American Lutheran Church: hospitals, homes, etc. The part which concerns services to the aged is on pages 13-14. "To preserve for the aged person a place of dignity and love in society, to insure his right to be a person, and to enable him to be a contributing human being as long as possible—these are the goals of services to the aging in the ALC."

121. App, Austin J. The Catholic stake in the aged: The role of religion in the case of older people. *Social Justice Review,* January 1959, *51,* 291-93.

Man is "incurably religious." And yet, the majority of secular and governmental projects for the aged are carried on as if man lived by bread alone and had no soul, no hereafter. In 1958, there were 314 Catholic homes for the aged, with 27,890 guests. Add the elderly patients treated in Catholic hospitals, and the Catholic stake in old persons is a great one.

122. Baptista, Sister Maria. A missing generation in Catholic charities. *Catholic Charities Review,* February 1961, *45,* 5-10.

The development of a Special Services to Older Persons unit in Catholic Family Counseling, Inc., originated in a conviction that the needs and problems of older persons were not adequately understood by all caseworkers, simply by virtue of their graduate training in a school of social work. Older persons must be helped to maintain a satisfying self-image and to attain the greatest possible independence.

123. Beattie, Walter M. A research project in church services to the aging. *Review of Religious Research,* Winter 1963, *4* (2), 104-16.

The St. Louis Metropolitan Health and Welfare Council worked with religious communities to identify ways in which churches could minister to the aging. This article was written just as the research project was getting under way. Subheadings: Church Approaches under Challenge, A Research Project for St. Louis, Some Methodological Problems, Study of Target Congregations, Beginnings. The "eight principles of action research" on pages 105 and 106 are considered basic.

124. Berman, Rochel, & Geis, Ellen. Intergenerational contact: Theological and social insights. *Religious Education*, 1975, 70, 661-75.

Young people from a college in New York state made contact with residents at Riverdale Hebrew Home for the Aged. This article describes: the theological and sociological framework; the college students, who were single, Roman Catholic, and sixteen in number; the findings (students' anticipation of their own aging, acceptance or rejection of old age, feelings about institutionalized care, discovery of the elderly, concentration on a death-and-dying course). Implications are drawn for future study.

125. Bernadette de Lourdes, Mother Mary. *Where somebody cares.* New York: Putnam and Sons, 1959.

This book is a very detailed account of the genesis, building, and administration of the Mary Manning Walsh Home for the Aged in New York City, run by a Catholic Carmelite Order of Sisters. Special services described include psychological and occupational therapy, geriatric health, speech and hearing therapy.

126. Bier, William C. (Ed.). *Aging: Its challenge to the individual and to society.* New York: Fordham University Press, 1974.

This volume contains the 26 papers presented at one of the biennial "institutes" in pastoral psychology at the Jesuit university of Fordham in New York. Topics span the whole field of aging, not just its religious aspects. The book is cited here principally as an instance of church interest in the whole field of aging; several individual themes are noted elsewhere in this bibliography.

127. Biller, Newman M. The role of the synagogue in work with old people. *Jewish Social Services Quarterly*, 1952, 28 (3), 284-89.

Historically, the synagogue has always inspired a reverent attitude towards the old and a sense of duty to provide for them in case of need. Longevity was regarded in the Jewish tradition as a divine blessing and a human ambition. Homes for the poor and aged, as well as benevolent societies to care for them, were established in the Middle Ages. To help synagogues and rabbis discharge their duties, their article gives a description of older persons' special needs and offers suggestions as to how the synagogue can help.

128. Blakely, Thomas J. *A personal service program for senior adults.* Grand Rapids, Mich.: Diocesan Development Fund Services to Senior Adults, 1965. Mimeo; pages not numbered.

Contains chapters on: "The Senior Club," "Visiting," "Communications," "Errands," "Spiritual Services." The last-mentioned chapter comments briefly on the attitude of the senior adult towards religion: "Studies show that religious fervor and strength in faith actively increase with age. Recognition of the impending end of life, and the knowledge of a promised reward after death."

129. Boeddeker, Alfred. The Franciscan and the specialized needs of certain members of the family. *Franciscan Educational Conference,* 1960, *41,* 66-106.

A paper delivered at the 41st annual Franciscan Educational Conference at Quincy, Illinois, August 1960. Describes, among other things, the initiative of a Franciscan parish in San Francisco—Madonna Residence, with its Senior Citizens' Center. The residence is a hotel "for elderly ladies on reduced incomes."

130. Braun, Viola K. Older adults need fellowship. *International Journal of Religious Education,* Nov. 1953, *30,* 21-22.

Unlike children, whose days are filled with school and extracurricular interests, older adults have time on their hands and are eager and willing to use their leisure hours. They crave fellowship, a feeling of belonging, of being of use. Examples of fellowship groups: teas, folk games, tours, book reviews, weekly luncheon, monthly party. A checklist is provided for finding out "what are your interests?"

131. Brigh, Sister Mary, & Eymard, Sister M. The family and its aged members. *Franciscan Educational Conference,* 1960, *41,* 169-75.

Franciscan idealism and family responsibility for its aged members. How the aged can remain family centered and stay in their own homes through a Home Care Program. Concrete example of the Franciscan Sisters at St. Mary's Hospital in Rochester, Minnesota, establishing a program to care for the sick and the aged in their own homes. Group social activities were also introduced. As of 1960, each of the three Catholic parishes in Rochester had a parish apostolate to the aged.

132. Cameron, Paul. Valued aspects of religion to Negroes and Whites. *Proceedings, 77th Annual Convention of the American Psychological Association,* 1969, 741-42.

The Cameron Religious Dimensions Scale was administered to "a stratified area sample from 38 systematically drawn census tracts within the city of Detroit [yielding] 126 Negroes and 282 Whites between the ages of 12 and 99." However, a breakdown by age and race totals 121 Negroes, 4 of them over 64 years of age, and 284 Whites, 9 of them in the 64-and-over bracket. The one table offers no breakdown by age, but the writer does assert that, for both races, "the low point was generally between the ages of 25 and 35, and the high points were before 18, between the ages of 45-55, and after 68."

133. Catholic Bishops of America. Society and the aged: Toward reconciliation. *Origins,* May 20, 1976, *5* (48), 757-61.

(Citation 133 continued)
Declaration of the American Catholic Bishops at their annual meeting in Chicago in 1976. The elderly have human rights, which include: a right to life, to a decent income, to employment, to medical care, to food, to decent housing, to equal treatment. The role of the church is explored, as is the role of individuals, that of families, and that of communities. The church is seen as an advocate for public policy.

134. Catholic Bishops of Canada.   Honor for the aged. (Intervention, Synod of Bishops, Rome.) *Origins*, October 30, 1980, *10* (20), 313-14.

In a written "intervention" (speech) at the International Synod of Catholic Bishops at Rome, the Canadian delegates stressed the unique contribution of wisdom which the elderly can make to the family and to society. If the biblical commandment to honor father and mother should fail to evoke a filial response, pragmatic considerations might prevail. There are obvious implications for economic policies.

135. Catholic Charities.   News notes of the Commission on the Aging: National Conference of Catholic Charities. *Catholic Charities Review*, February 1964, *48*, 18.

Purpose and membership of the national Catholic Commission on the Aging which held its first meeting in Chicago in December 1963. Its aims: (a) to define the Catholic philosophy of service to the aging, (b) to identify and accredit institutions and agencies serving the aged, (c) to plan a five-to-ten-year program of various services under Catholic auspices.

136. Catholic Digest.   December 1972, *37* (2), 72-96.

This issue features five articles on aging, condensed from various newspapers and periodicals: "Aging: What's the Problem?" by Rose DeWolf and Harriet Watson; "Rose Kennedy Keeps Blooming," by Lenore Hershey; "The First 37,109 Days of Salvatore Tarascio," by Berry Stainback; "When Sisters Retire, It's Work, Work, Work" by Dorothy Townsend; "Maria, Joe, and Project HEAD," by Vicky Peralta.

137. Chakerian, Charles G. (Ed.).   *The aging and the United Presbyterian Church in the USA*. New York: U.P. Board of Missions, Division of Health and Welfare, 1965.

Contains the following papers: "The Church and Community in Relation to Older People," by Walter Beattie; "The Church's Social Service to the Individual and the Family," by Sue W. Spencer; "The Church's Role in the Provision of Housing," by Lawrence Upton; "The Church and Its Role in the Promotion of Health in Older Persons," by Prescott Thompson; "Theological Implications of the Problem of Aging," by Herbert Lazenby; "Psychological Aspects of Aging," by Francis Braceland, M.D.; "Issues and

Recommendations of the United Presbyterian Consultation on the Aging,"
by John McDowell.

138. Cody, John Cardinal. Growing with the years: A pastoral letter of
the Archbishop of Chicago. *Osservatore Romano* (English ed.), June 27, 1974,
26 (326), 10-11.

The "holy year" with its emphasis on healing draws attention to concern
for the aging. Five "wounds" are identified which call for healing: (a) indifference to old people's need for physical care, (b) failing to understand that
their needs are more than just physical, (c) assuming that the young do not
need the old, (d) financial insecurity, (e) alienation. The wounds can be healed
by recognizing the good example of the aged, their precious gift of time to be
enjoyed, their independence to speak their thoughts honestly.

139. Cook, C. J., & Saxon, S. J. Guide for forming senior citizens'
groups. *Catholic Charities Review*, December 1960, *44*, 29-31.

In the diocese of Toledo, Ohio, the Society of St. Vincent de Paul joined
with Catholic Charities in seeking to establish a senior citizens' club in every
parish. Suggestions: Do not be discouraged if only a few show up at the first
meeting. Do not expect more than one-third of the group to be men. Keep
the meetings short because elderly people tire more easily.

140. Cook, Thomas C., Jr. (Ed.). *The religious sector explores its mission in
aging.* Athens, Ga.: National Interfaith Coalition on Aging, 1976.

A report, representing the combined efforts of a number of religious
bodies, on programs for the aging under religious auspices. Part 1 is about
the project and its methodology; part 2 is about the data; part 3 is on education. There are four appendices and a useful survey of the literature on
religion and aging (pp. 117-29). The annotated bibliography of more than
100 entries aims at updating Maves' work in Tibbitts' *Handbook of Social
Gerontology.* A total of 111 religious organizations participated in the NICA
survey, which covered 1,577 programs in 48 states and 4 Canadian pro-
vinces. Collectively, the participating denominations represent a "constituency" of 262,766 congregations.

141. Culver, Elsie Thomas. *New church programs with the aging.* New
York: Associated Press, 1961.

A very useful little book for the practitioners who deal with the elderly.
Contents: Growing Older in a New World, Religious Education for Maturity,
Effects of Aging and of Religion on Health, Worship and Counsel, Older
People Need Fun Too, Action Groups and Ballot Boxes, The Wholeness of
Life. Appendix A is on the church's responsibility to older persons: a memo
to the churches. Appendix B brings some basic statistics. Appendix C is a
bibliography on aging.

142. Defois, Gérard. La pastorale des personnes âgées: Document de la commission nationale française des personnes âgées. *La Documentation Catholique* [Paris], June 20, 1976, 73, 569-71.

The French National Catholic Commission for the Aged, created in 1970, has published various studies and statements on the problem. This is an outline of pastoral care for the aged.

143. Demmy, Michael, & Trifiro, Anthony. Today's teens comfort yesterday's children. *Our Sunday Visitor*, May 15, 1977, 66, 8-9.

A parochial school in Norwich, New York, has an "adopted grandparent" program. Each Wednesday afternoon, ninth graders visit the elderly residents of an extended care facility. This program benefits the elderly while it also helps the young. Patients are reminded of the world around them and feel they are still part of it. Photos.

144. Diocesan pension plans (for lay employees). *Social Justice Review*, May 1962, 55, 58-59.

Among the news notes entitled "Social Review," there is a short notice stating that several Catholic dioceses in the U.S.A. were putting in pension plans for their lay employees. The archdiocese of New York put its plan into effect on July 1, 1962.

145. Douglas, Margaret. Serving the lonely aging. *Catholic Charities Review*, April 1965, 49, 13-17.

To assist the elderly in remaining self-sufficient in their own homes, the San Francisco Archdiocesan Catholic Committee for the Aging has been developing and promoting programs to satisfy the needs of the elderly. Particular stress has been laid on programs administered at the parish level. A visiting program by lay people is described. Thirteen Catholic high schools are having students visit 20 different hospitals and homes for the aged. One center serves single men living in the skid-row hotels of downtown San Francisco; membership, 150 men.

146. Faist, Russell L. The church and the aging. *Ave Maria*, January 7, 1961, 93 (1), 20-23.

This article contains some data on what the Catholic church in America was doing for the aging prior to 1961. If offers highlights on Monsignor Raymond Gallagher, coordinator of all Catholic participation in the First White House Conference on the Aging in 1961.

147. Ferenstein, Barbara Collins. How your church works for you. *Harvest Years*, 1967, 7 (4), 6-11.

Churches and religious organizations offer many forms of service to the elderly, including housing, recreation, health and welfare assistance, and learning opportunities.

148. Ford, Robert A.   How Catholics can cooperate with homes for the aging. *Catholic Charities Review*, June 1961, *45*, 3-5.

Between Catholic Charities of New York and 10 Catholic homes for the aged, there are five areas of cooperation: (a) helping to implement state and city rules for such homes; (b) implementing the suggestions of the Department of Welfare; (c) liaison with all public and private agencies which relate to these homes; (d) sponsoring workshops for personnel; (e) studying problems that relate to the future, given the acute growth of the aging population.

149. Gaffney, Sister Marie.   *Growing old.* Chicago: Claretian Publications, 1972.

On the importance and the special needs of older Americans. The physical, psychological, practical, social, and religious needs of the aging. Out of 120 Roman Catholic dioceses which answered a survey, 77 have people especially assigned to work with the elderly. Twenty-five have a special department on aging, and 40 have designated a professional for this work.

150. Gallagher, Raymond.   The Commission on Aging: National Conference of Catholic Charities. *Catholic Charities Review*, January 1964, *48*, 2-3.

An editorial on the establishment of a national Catholic Commission on the Aging in December 1963. Steering groups and subcommittees are developing a philosophy of service to the aging with definite goals. A variety of programs was expected to come out of this commission.

151. Gallagher, Raymond J., Tannenbaum, Marc H., & Villaume, William J.   *White House Conference on Aging 1961, background papers: No. 15: Religion and Aging. No. 20: Services of religious groups for the aging.* Washington, D.C.: U.S. Govt. Printing Office, Nov. 1960, total pp.: 38.

Two background papers which were prepared for the 1961 White House Conference on Aging, under the direction of the committee for "Religion and Aging." The three clergymen listed as authors here were the cochairmen of this committee. The first paper listed above (#15) sets forth the basic philosophical concepts agreed upon by the committee; the second (#20) lists various services provided by the churches and synagogues.

152. GCA World. The official magazine of Catholic Golden Age.

Volume 1, number 1 appeared in January/February 1981. It is intended as a bimonthly publication for this 600,000-member group for Catholics who are 50 years of age and over. The address is: Suite 300, Scranton Life Building, Scranton, PA 18503.

153. Gleason, George.   *Horizons for older people.* New York: Macmillan Co., 1956.

(Citation 153 continued)

Written for elderly people, but even more, for those pastors and church leaders who are seeking answers to such questions as "What are the needs of the older adults in our community?" and "How can our church help meet these needs?" Church groups, meeting personal needs, serving the church and the community. The eight appendices contain a bibliography, a list of Protestant and nonchurch homes for the aged. No Catholic or Jewish homes are mentioned.

154. Goetz, Howard C., Jr. (Ed.). *Manual for senior citizens' programming.* New Orleans: Greater New Orleans Federation of Churches and the Louisiana Commission on the Aging, 1968.

Typescript format, bound into a book, half an inch thick, the pages [approximately 120 of them] are not numbered consecutively, but only section by section. The 15 sections in the book are as follows: Introduction, The Church and the Aging, The Leaders, Needs of the Aging, Understanding the Aging, The Elderly and the Community, Volunteers, Health Maintenance, Programs, Social and Referral Services, Employment for Aging, Protective Services, Multi-service Centers, Promotion and Financing, Pre-retirement Training.

155. The golden age club. [Parish-directed social, spiritual, and economic help.] *Priest,* October 1959, *15,* 821-25.

Suggests that a parish priest can help senior citizens socially, spiritually, and materially. A senior citizens' club, meeting one afternoon a week for recreation and lunch, can help social relationships of the elderly. Mail them the weekly bulletin; arrange to have parish societies visit them.

156. Guides for Catholic Homes for the Aging. Washington, D.C.: National Conference of Catholic Charities, 1964.

The report defines the purposes and the guiding policies of Catholic Homes for the Aging. It suggests steps to be taken in planning a new or enlarged home and describes the services and duties of each staff member. Emphasis is placed on obtaining for the resident whatever he needs for his full security and well-being. Various services are described: social services, medical and nursing care, physical and occupational therapy, nutrition and dietary service, leisure-time activities, religious attention.

157. Hafrey, Daniel J. Presbyterian village. *Geriatrics,* 1959, *14,* 728-33.

This article describes a Presbyterian home for the aged in New York: its activities, arrangements, other features. The village covers 34 acres and houses 60 persons, with plans for expansion to accommodate 500. It illustrates what one religious body is doing for the elderly. Photos.

158. Harrington, Janette, & Webb, Muriel S. *Who cares?* New York: Friendship Press, 1962.

A "project guidebook on the church's mission and persons in special need." Chapter 2 is entitled, "Aging—Handicap or Opportunity?" Other chapters in the book deal with other groups: handicapped children, the physiologically handicapped, and persons with emotional disturbances. Chapter 5 is on "Theology and Mission"; Chapter 6 is on "Evaluation and the Future."

159. H.E.A.D. [Help Elderly Adults Direct]. Harrisburg: Pennsylvania Catholic Conference, Gold Ribbon Committee on Aging, 1973, typescript.

"A formula for mobilizing churches in a social action community-based program with the elderly." Subdivisions: What Is Project H.E.A.D.?, Why Project H.E.A.D.?, Methodology (in five steps), The Six-Point Program, Some Examples, The Challenge, Background of the Challenge, An Invitation to an Opportunity, Conclusion, Survey Form Used, Questions Often Asked about Project H.E.A.D. and Some Answers to Them, Training Program Outline.

160. Heinecken, Martin, & Hellerich, Ralph. *The church's ministry with older adults: A theological basis.* New York: Lutheran Church in America, Division for Mission in North America, 1976.

A document in which the Lutheran Church in America (LCA) seeks to outline its ministry to the aging, to set up its goals, and to provide a theological basis for such work.

161. Hiltner, Seward (Ed.). *Toward a theology of aging.* New York: Human Sciences Press, 1975, 1-181. NB: This was a special issue of *Pastoral Psychology*, Winter 1974, 24 (229).

Papers and discussion from an ecumenical workshop to consider the implications of theology for older people and for the process of aging itself. This workshop was held at Saint Paul's Theological Seminary in Kansas City, Missouri, in May of 1974. Participants were drawn from Catholic, Protestant, and Jewish theological seminaries. The "Discussion and Comment" by Seward Hiltner (pp. 168-74) both summarizes the small groups' discussions and adds his own reflections.

162. Hixenbaugh, Elinor R. Apostles to the aging. *Catholic Charities Review*, May 1959, *43* (5), 16-19.

How the needs of the elderly are being met in the parishes of Rochester, Minnesota; Buffalo, New York; and Youngstown, Ohio: Visiting, reading, writing letters, helping with housework, shopping. Catholic Charities of New York has set up a special unit for the aging within its Family Service Division; this new unit supervises group work activities in day centers and in homes for the aged. Detroit Catholic Charities has a Department for the Aging, with concrete activities listed in this article. St. Mary's Hospital in Rochester, Minnesota provides a home nursing service.

163. Hoeffner, J. Cardinal. Le sens chrétien du troisième âge. *La Documentation Catholique* (Paris), April 6, 1975, *72*, 330-33.

Original in German. The Catholic Archibishop of Cologne issues a pastoral letter concerning the elderly and concerning the Christian meaning of old age.

164. Hofmeister, G. Religion 'ist Privatsache'? Sinnfragen und Sinngebung im Rahmen einer überkonfessionellen Bildungseinrichtung für ältere Menschen. *Zeitschrift für Gerontologie*, Jan.-Feb. 1977, *10* (1), 43-50.

Sandkrughof bei Lauenburg/Elbe, a nondenominational facility for senior citizens since 1974 has been offering religious themes as a part of its overall program which give meaning to old age and encourage the elderly to live a full life.

165. Hover, Margot K. Family ministry—the elderly. *Marriage*, April 1980, *62*, 10-13.

Description of a training program set up to foster greater responsiveness to the elderly on the part of parish families in Visitation Catholic Church in Kansas City, Missouri. The program lasted three months, one session per week, and also involved some of the elderly along with the "host families."

166. Jacobs, H. Lee. *Senior citizens in the church and community* (3d ed.). Iowa City: State University of Iowa Institute of Gerontology, 1960.

The second revision of a booklet originally published under the title of *Senior Citizens in Church and Community.* The aim of all the booklets was to provide individuals, groups, and churches with basic information on aging, along with some practical suggestions on how to help retired persons to remain participating members of their respective communities. This third edition, revising a 33-page one of 1958, was prepared under the sponsorship of both the Institute of Gerontology and the School of Religion at the State University of Iowa.

167. Jewish Women. *Continuing choices: A comprehensive handbook of programs for work with older adults.* New York: National Council of Jewish Women, 1975.

This guide for use by volunteers describes 48 different programs of service to the aged.

168. John Paul II. Love and Respect for the Aged. *L'Osservatore Romano,* English Edition, January 8, 1979, No. 2 (563 in consecutive numbering), 12.

This is a five-minute homily which the Pope addressed to some 40,000 people gathered in St. Peter's Square in Rome. Those of advanced age, he said, are sometimes forsaken; they must be respected and not treated as if they were now useless.

169. John Paul II. Address to the Participants in the International Forum on Active Aging: About the Special Ministry of the Elderly in the Life of the Human Family. *L'Osservatore Romano*, English Edition, January 8, 1979, No. 38 (650 in consecutive numbering), 3.

The aging are a part of God's plan for the world. They are encouraged to look upon their role with realism and serenity. It is praiseworthy to support initiatives on their behalf, to defend their right to life and to promote their special mission in the human family. Old age is able to enrich the world through prayer and counsel; its capacity for evangelization by word and example is a force for the Church of God yet to be understood or adequately utilized.

170. Kader, Raymond A. *Senior adult utilization and ministry handbook.* Nashville: Broadman Press, 1974.

This handbook, which is about the size and shape of a news magazine, is described on its cover as a practical guide for utilizing the many talents of senior adults, for ministering to them, for ministering to shut-ins and nursing home senior adults, and for organizing senior adult programs for any size church. Although brief, this booklet should be helpful for those actually working with the elderly. The bulk of the material is made up of 22 "figures, charts, surveys, and forms" which make for easy reading and ready comprehension.

171. Kalson, Leon. Kosher meals-on-wheels. *Gerontologist*, 1974, *14* (1), 33-34.

This article describes the development of Kosher Meals-on-Wheels as a specific outreach of the Jewish Home and Hospital for the Aged in Pittsburgh. Criteria for acceptance into the program are discussed, as well as the social and psychological benefits flowing from it.

172. Lee, William M. A parish program for the aged. *Catholic Charities Review*, May 1960, *44* (5), 27-28.

Concerns the Golden Age Club sponsored by Sacred Heart Parish in Pittsburgh. Organized in 1956, it meets on Friday afternoon; membership is open to all parishioners aged 60 and over. The Golden Age Club has stimulated interest and participation in the overall functioning of the parish.

173. Legan, Kathryn. *Activities for older adults in a sampling of Milwaukee County churches and synagogues.* Milwaukee: Interfaith Program for the Elderly, 1977, typescript.

The purpose of this study was to identify older adult groups and activities existing in the sampling referred to and to determine existing and potential volunteer groups in religious institutions. The Interfaith Program for the Elderly is a neighborhood-based, interdenominational program which seeks to cooperate with churches and synagogues in working with and for the elderly. Included is a directory of Milwaukee-area religious institutions with neighborhood activities for the elderly.

174. Lutheran Church in America. *Aging and the older adult.* Chicago, 1978.

Headings: Aging, Prejudice, and Injustice, Theological Affirmations, Agenda for Action (families, congregations, theological seminaries, retirement policies of this church, public policy), Conclusion. Adopted by the 9th biennial convention at Chicago, July 12-19, 1978.

175. Madden, Declan. Senior roadrunners: A parish program for golden years. *Today's Parish,* Nov.-Dec. 1977, 9 (8), 16-17.

The author regularly visits ten nursing homes a week for Mass, communion, and a friendly visit. Seeing the people always idle, he hired two buses for a trip in November of 1970. At the time of writing, with nondenominational support, the so-called "Senior Roadrunners" were chartering 23 buses a month to take the elderly from Metropolitan Denver for a ride, for a trip to some local tourist spot, or for a tour through nearby parts of the state.

176. Maves, Paul B. The church in community planning for the aged. *Geriatrics,* Nov.-Dec. 1950, 5, 339-42.

What role should the church play on the geriatric team? How could the church contribute to community planning for the aged? To answer these questions, the functions of religion are briefly analyzed and the role of the church is identified as: (a) goal setting and value setting; (b) stimulating the community planning to implement these goals and values; (c) cooperating with other agencies in securing necessary resources which older people may need in handling their conflicts, resolving tensions, and achieving adequate satisfaction.

177. Maves, Paul B. *The Christian religious education of older people.* New York: Federal Council of Churches of Christ in America, 1950.

This is written with successive chapters devoted to the problem, to basic assumptions, to the method, to the data, and to conclusion and comments. It studies thirteen Protestant churches. The thesis is that religious education of older people is an important and integral part of total ministry and that the churches' programs for this purpose are not so effective as they should be.

178. Maves, Paul B. Aging, religion, and the church. In Tibbitts, Clark (Ed.). *Handbook of Social Gerontology; Societal Aspects of Aging.* Chicago: Univ. of Chicago Press, 1960, 698-749.

Questions are asked about religion and aging and about the impact of aging on the churches. Factors which complicate the study are pointed out.

Theoretical considerations are offered about religion, about Judeo-Christian attitudes regarding old age and aging. Included is a historical sketch of the way religious bodies cared for the aged. There is a description of church programs for older people and of older people's participation in them, some early research on the subject, national surveys, Catholic parish research, community studies; the meaning of religion, participation, isolation; concluding observations and hypotheses.

179. Meier, Levi. Filial responsibility to the senile parent: A Jewish approach. *Journal of Psychology and Judaism,* 1977, 2 (1), 45-53.

In the Jewish tradition, behavior towards one's parents is governed by two concepts: (a) honor, or *kibbud,* which is defined as positive acts of personal service; and (b) reverence, or *morah,* which is the avoidance of disrespectful acts. The purpose of this paper is to explore the Talmud and Maimonides to see whether these obligations still hold when one's parent is senile. The child's responsibility is not altered if the parent behaves abnormally, but Maimonides makes exceptions when the parent is mentally disturbed. Then the child is exempt from personal service to the parent, but not from responsibility to ensure the parent's being cared for by others.

180. Mershon, James Merwyn. Aging, and a model program for older persons in the church. *Dissertation Abstracts International,* September 1979, *40* (3-A), 1527.

The problem posed was how the church might be helpful in meeting the needs of the aging. Specifically, the author sought to ascertain the needs of senior citizens in the 4,500-member University Church of the Seventh-Day Adventists in Loma Linda, California. Subsequently, three organizational units were established to meet social needs, lifetime learning needs, and "the outreach of serving others in continuing valued self-giving." Attention was paid to the recruiting and training of volunteers. One major finding of the programs was that the church is in a special position to offer significance in life satisfaction experiences, in deepening personal identity, and in the spiritual value of the assurance of life beyond this life. Each person is of inestimable value, regardless of age. (School of Theology at Claremont, 1979.)

181. Mills, B. M. *The educational interests and needs of older adults in selected Presbyterian churches* (Ed.D dissertation). Ann Arbor: University of Michigan Press, 1968.

An attempt is made to distinguish between the felt needs and the real needs of Presbyterians over the age of 65; also, to discover how ministers identify such needs and interests; finally, the implications for adult religious education. Of 235 older adults, 30% indicated some educational need, such as Bible study; of 47 ministers, 59% tried to ascertain the needs of the aged, mostly by asking the aged person. Conclusions: the elderly need to understand later life development tasks, to improve verbal communication, and to respect diversity within the church.

182. Ministry with the aging. *Austin Seminary Bulletin* (faculty ed.), October 1980, 96 (3), 1-41.

This number of the faculty edition bulletin published by the Austin Presbyterian Theological Seminary is devoted almost entirely to the subject of ministry to the aging. Its contents are: "Introduction," by Jack M. Maxwell; "Letter to a New Pastor," by Bert Kruger Smith; "Pastoral Care with the Elderly," by Ralph L. Underwood; "The Church's Educational Ministry with the Aging," by David Ng; "First Southern Presbyterian Church—One Look at Ministry with Aging People," by J. Carter King III. There is a one-page bibliography "For Further Reading," and a list of seven "Referrals," which are addresses from which information can be obtained.

183. Moberg, David O. The integration of older members in the church congregation. In Rose, A. M., & Peterson, W. A., *Older people and their social world.* Philadelphia: F. A. Davis Co., 1965, 125-40.

This study explores the problems of integration of the aged into the mainstream of associational life. It is better for them to be integrated rather than segregated from younger people. Yet, where integration reigns in a congregation, a neglect of the aged is a common result. Calling attention to the needs of the aged through specialized programs does single out and segregate the elderly. Desires expressed by the elderly were for transportation, visits of shut-ins, activities that are useful as well as recreational, recognition for past services. Evidence was found of an emerging subculture of the aging.

184. Mosely, J. Edward. The many faces of aging. St. Louis: Christian Board of Publications, n.d.

Published under the auspices of the Disciples of Christ, this booklet discusses church service to the aged and some patterns and resources.

185. Murphy, Joseph, & Walters, Frank J. Setting up an archdiocesan pension plan. *Catholic Property Administration,* April 1963, 27, 30-33.

In the early 1960s few if any of America's Catholic dioceses had a pension plan to protect their employees in old age. The vast New York Archdiocese was one of the first to establish one. This article gives a detailed description of the process, from the first recommendation by the Archdiocesan Board of Consultors in September 1961, to the appointment of a trustee in December 1962. Given the complexity of the archdiocese and its varied institutions, this was a major undertaking, interesting from a historical standpoint as well as being a model for many similar ventures. (See also citations 187, 197.)

186. National Lutheran Council. *Guide for Lutheran social welfare agencies for services to the aging.* New York: National Lutheran Council, Division of Welfare, 1960.

(Citation 186 continued)

This booklet considers Lutheran agency services to old people as related to the individual and his or her community, to homes for the aging, and to congregations. It was "written with the conviction that aging services to older people can be enlarged and improved and in the expectation that it will stimulate thought and action in their behalf."

187. New York's forward look: Archdiocesan pension plan. *Ave Maria*, May 5, 1962, 95, 17.

The pension plan of the Catholic Archdiocese of New York, effective July 1, 1962, provides 20,000 lay employees with an annual income of 50 to 75% of their salary upon retirement. (See also citations 185, 197.)

188. Ng, David. The church's educational ministry with the aging. *Austin Seminary Bulletin* (faculty ed.), Oct. 1980, 96 (3), 23-30.

After two pages of "wisdom about old age," the writer offers a rationale for educational ministry with the aging and closes with a section on "What can a church do?" Eight practical concerns are suggested which a church ought to keep in view when developing its program for the aging.

189. Northern California-Nevada: News of the Christian world. *Christian Century*, 1960, 76 (44), 1293.

The Northern California & Nevada Council of Churches urges its local member churches to take part in the San Francisco conference on "Aging with a future." Churches are encouraged to help in housing, care, and fellowship, to be aware of physical and psychological changes associated with aging.

190. Oakland Council of Churches. *The church at work.* Oakland: Oakland Council of Churches, Social Service Bureau, 1966.

There are two mimeographed booklets with the same "Church at Work" title: (a) "A Proposal Embracing a Community-wide Plan for Providing Low-cost Housing and Supporting Social Services to Low-income Elderly Persons" (16 pp.); and (b) "A Proposal for a Senior Activity Component" (2 pp.).

191. O'Donnell, P. Why not more Catholic old folks' homes? *Homiletic and Pastoral Review*, 1963, 63, 378; 441-42.

Using 1963 costs and figures, the writer argued that a million-dollar old folks' home housing 240 people could be paid off in 40 years and would then begin to operate at a profit of $73,000 a year. Cost changes over two decades date this article.

192. Ogle, Alice. Little miracle hotel. *Marianist*, June 1961, 54, 29-31.

This is a popularly written account of a San Francisco hotel, redone under the leadership of a Catholic priest to "give elderly women the opportunity to live in simple dignity." To be eligible, a woman must be at least 60 years old and sufficiently active to take care of herself. At the time of writing, there were 76 guests, and the rent for a single room was $5 a week.

193. Old age in a Christian perspective. *Modern Liturgy,* May 1979, 6, 8-15.

The May 1979 number of *Modern Liturgy* magazine was planned from the perspective of liturgy and the elderly. There are four short articles on this theme: "Where have all the elders gone?" by Eileen E. Freeman; "A celebration of retirement," by Brian McAloon; "Rise up in honor before the hoary head," by Eileen E. Freeman; "I'd rather fight than switch!" by Residents of Sun City, Arizona, reacting to the post-Vatican II Catholic liturgy (short paragraphs from various elderly residents).

194. Older adults and the church. Atlanta: Presbyterian Church in the United States, Office of Adult Education, 1963.

A manual on how to start an older adult fellowship group and how to carry out a program for the elderly. There is a plan for use with shut-ins, as well as a bibliography for the Christian education worker.

195. Packard, George F. A church houses the elderly. In Boyd, Rosamonde Ramsey, & Oakes, Charles G. (Eds.). *Foundations of practical gerontology.* Columbia: Univ. of S. Carolina Press, 1969, 211-15.

Relates what was done by St. Mary's Episcopal Church in Baltimore to provide housing for the elderly. Another edition was published in 1973.

196. The Particular Council [of the St. Vincent de Paul Society] and the aging. *Catholic Charities Review,* November 1959, 43, 28.

Lansing's Particular Council of the St. Vincent de Paul Society focused the attention of local conferences on the problems of the aging. All members, it was emphasized, should understand social security benefits and have some knowledge about the medical and legal advice which elderly persons might need. Stress was laid on the necessity of visiting elderly persons in convalescent homes, institutions, or in their own homes. In each parish, the need for a drop-in center or a club for elderly persons must be studied.

197. Pension plan for lay employees: New York Archdiocese. *Catholic School Journal,* September 1962, 62, 96.

The pension plan of the Archdiocese of New York, in effect on July 1, 1962, covers 20,000 lay persons employed in 402 parishes, 423 schools, 193 hospitals, agencies, and welfare institutions of the Archdiocese. Together with social security benefits, the pension plan is expected to provide the employee with 50 to 75% of his or her salary on retirement. (See also citations 185, 187.)

198. Peralta, V. Maria, Joe, and Project HEAD. *Catholic Digest*, December 1972, *37*, 93-96.

The neighborhood church can be the most useful of all institutions which help the elderly to help themselves. Any person, priest, or minister can implement Project HEAD (Help Elderly Adults Direct). Five basic steps are involved.

199. Peralta, Vicky. *Join Operation HEAD* (Self help for the aging). (Rev. Ed.). Philadelphia: Catholic Social Services, 1974.

Introduction, What Is Operation HEAD?, Methodology in Five Steps, The Six-Point Program, Some Examples (Maria and Joe), The Challenge, Background of the Challenge, An Invitation to an Opportunity, Survey Form.

200. Pistrui, William. Nazareth Retired Sisters Home. *Hospital Progress*, May 11, 1963, *44*, 107.

A description by the architect of a new convent-hospital facility designed to serve the spiritual and physical needs of 160 retired Sisters. Located in St. Louis County, Missouri. Useful as an illustration of the way in which a building must be adapted to the physical limitations of its occupants.

201. Pitrone, Jean Madden. Campus living for older people: Rochford Terrace, Detroit. *Ave Maria*, September 28, 1963, 98 (13), 20-23.

In 1954, the Catholic Archdiocese of Detroit purchased a deteriorating social hall near the church of St. John Nepomucene in downtown Detroit to make it into an activity center for senior citizens. The Project grew to include residences dedicated in 1963. At the time of writing, there were 103 people living at the "Kundig Center" and about 1,500 more who come to join in the various center activities.

202. Poteat, Gordon. The ministry of organized religion to the aged. In Scudder, Delton (Ed.), *Organized religion and the older person*. Gainesville: Univ. of Florida Press, 1958, 43-52.

Despite the general wording of the chapter title, this paper is simply a description of what one local church (The Tourist Church of Daytona Beach) is doing for senior citizens. Women's Association, Women's Service Guild, Weekly Study Hour, Sunday Worship, Funerals, Visiting Homes and Hospitals.

203. Presbyterian Church in the USA. *Homes for the aging.* Typescript, April 1971.

A three-page listing of homes for the aging in the USA which are related to the Presbyterian church. Name, address, city, telephone number, name of director. At the time the directory was drawn up, there were about 35 in all, with several more under construction.

204. Presbyterian Church in the U.S.A. *Older persons in the church program.* Philadelphia: Presbyterian Church in the USA, 1957.

A popularly written booklet to assist local churches in providing a program of Christian education that will include the older persons in the congregation. It contains chapters on the needs and interests of old people, on how to organize a club, on pastoral ministries, on other related topics.

205. Quaker Life Magazine, July 1961, Series II (7).

This special issue on aging contains the following relevant articles: "Friends Care for the Aged," by Murray C. Johnson; "Quaker Forum: How Can the Society Care for Aging Friends?" by R. Ernest Lamb and Florence Tobiessen; "Retirement and a Second Career," by Muriel Chamoulaud; "Have You Considered the Pension Plan?" by Benjamin Wegesa; "Pacific Friends Home Proposed," by Rega Engelsberg; "Institution for Senile Friends under Study," by Charles Darlington. The address of the editorial office is 101 Quaker Hill Drive, Richmond IN 47374.

206. Rasmussen, Will C. The aging: Outreach services provided by congregation and community. *Lutheran Social Concern,* Summer 1972, *12* (2), 28-39.

Subheadings in the article: Goals to Be Achieved by Having Outreach Services; Outreach; An Activity That Requires Involvement; Plan for Action; The Congregation; a Grass Roots Organization; Outreach Services Facilitate Change; Groups and Outreach Services; Are Outreach Services Social Services?; Education; Nursing Home Consultation; Finding a Doctor; Companion Sitters; Chore Services; Shopping Services; Friendly Visiting and Assurance; Transportation Services; Library Service; Information and Referral; Legal Services; Outreach Service and the Volunteer; A Congregational Model of Outreach; Outreach Program Development.

207. Retirement programs for religious in the United States. The Secondary School Department of the National Catholic Educational Association, July 1977, 32.

In the spring of 1976, the National Conference of Catholic Bishops conducted a survey of all dioceses regarding their provisions for the reimbursement and retirement of religious. At the same time, the Leadership Conference of Women Religious and the Conference of Major Superiors of Men surveyed their membership to determine the source of monies utilized for retirement funds. This report analyzes the results of the surveys.

208. Rismiller, Arthur P. *Older members in the congregation.* Minneapolis: Augsburg Publishing House, 1964.

This book presents some material which churches may use as a guide in their programs of service to the elderly. It is intended for lay workers primarily, though not exclusively. The author served as a geriatrics chaplain for the Lutheran Welfare League in Columbus, Ohio.

209. Rodney, Bernard. The sacrament that honors old age. *Liguorian*, March 1975, 63 (3), 52-53.

The Catholic rite of the anointing of the sick may also be used for those suffering the infirmities of old age. It implies that the aged, even in their elder years, are and may be consecrated anew. A ceremony such as the one described in this article, with prayers for the aging and the sick, enhances the sense of self-value of those who take part in it, surrounded by ministers, singers, and "sponsors."

210. Salvation Army. *Golden Ager camp study.* New York: The Salvation Army, 1965.

History and evaluation of Golden Ager camping, which started in 1961. Types of programs, camp administration, recommendations.

211. Schaller, Lyle E. Church sponsorship of housing. *Journal of Housing*, 1966, 4, 195-99.

At the time he wrote this article, the writer was Director of the Regional Church Planning Office, an interdenominational agency serving fourteen Protestant churches in the Cleveland-Akron area. There is a short synopsis of church housing history, followed by a discussion of six issues such as accepting government subsidies, financing church-related projects, etc.

212. Sessoms, Robert L. *150 ideas for activities with senior adults.* Nashville: Broadman Press, 1977.

From the dusk jacket: "Out of many years of rich experience in working with [senior adults], Bob Sessoms shares practical suggestions for creative activities. Church leaders who already work with seniors will find this an invaluable tool. Pastors and other leaders in churches without senior adult activities will find helpful guidance on how to begin a program."

213. Singleton, Albert. Meals on wheels to the rescue. *Columbia* (Knights of Columbus Magazine), January 1981, 61 (1), 4-15.

This article, popularly written, describes the Meals on Wheels program in general, but particularly as it is operated in University City (St. Louis County), Missouri, by the Leisure Club of Christ the King Church and by the Knights of Columbus Duchesne Council of nearby Florissant, Missouri. Profusely illustrated.

214. Soete, Catherine J. A Pioneering Full-Service Agency for Older Americans: Cardinal Ritter Institute, St. Louis. *Hospital Progress*, August 1979, 60, 32-40.

(Citation 214 continued)

At Cardinal Ritter Institute, ways are sought to serve older men and women who do not need to be institutionalized but who do need some kind of help in order to live independently. More than half its annual budget goes for a home health care program; 25% towards volunteer and employment coordination, 19% for housing, and 3% goes into social services. Of patients treated by the home health care staff, 60% are more than 75 years old, 43% are between 75 and 84. Recently the institute's services were expanded to include a 180-bed nursing home, a nonprofit corporation supported by nine religious communities and by the CRI. The Institute also manages and staffs four apartment complexes and five housing projects owned by the St. Louis Housing Authority.

215. Spiritual well-being among Florida's older Lutherans. The Florida Lutheran Task Group on Aging of the Florida Lutheran Council on Social Ministry, 1976.

Three hundred older Lutherans living in Florida were interviewed on the question, "How well is the church serving the needs of the elderly who retire to Florida from all over the country?" These two reports by the Task Group tabulate and analyze the answers.

216. Spirituality and Aging: A Symposium. *Studies in Formative Spirituality*, November 1980, *1*, 331-92.

Volume I number 3 of this new journal published at Duquesne University is dedicated to spirituality and aging, though the first three articles are written from the vantage point of middle age. The table of contents offers short summaries of the articles, right after the title and the author's name: "Aging: Questions and the Quest" by Sister Germaine Hustedde; "The Second Journey" by Gerald O'Collins; "Reflections on the First Half of Mid-Life" by Sister Yvette Bellerose; "Maturing in the Lord: Reflections on Aging and the Spiritual Life" by Angelo M. Caligiuri; "Formative Perspectives on Life Review and Pastoral Counseling for the Elderly" by Richard K. Morcyz.

217. Stere, Patricia L. *The Lutheran church and the needs of the aged: A survey of the attitudes of members of the Susquehanna Region, Central Pennsylvania Synod.* Williamsport: Lycoming College, 1966.

One thousand Lutheran church members were polled on their attitudes toward the aged and on the Lutheran church's responsibility for meeting the needs of the aged. The poll population was drawn from 13 communities, urban, rural, and small town. The format of this study is the familiar one for a dissertation: review of the literature, hypotheses, method, findings, evaluation. Forty-five tables summarize the data collected; the questionnaire is found in the appendix. The aged formed 17% of the people questioned.

218. Stevenson, John Robert. The development of a lay ministry to elderly and shut-in members of the Rural Valley United Presbyterian Church. *Dissertation Abstracts International*, November 1980, *41* (5-A), 2161.

This paper attempts to develop a theological rationale for the D.Min. project described in the title. It goes on to discuss the problems of the elderly and describes the four training sessions held for seven callers. The results of the visits to the elderly are discussed, and there is an evaluation of the program. Rural Valley United Presbyterian Church is located in Armstrong County, Pennsylvania. (Drew University, 1980.)

219. St. Louis Health and Welfare Council Committee on Aging. *Project on churches and the aging: Working papers.* St. Louis: St. Louis Health and Welfare Council Committee on Aging, November 1962. Mimeographed.

Pages are not numbered consecutively, but when bound they make up a book half an inch thick. Robert C. Linstrom, project director, opens with a 12-page statement on the goals, organization, and procedures of the project, which is focused on determining the role of the church with older persons and on relating church programs to those of community health and welfare resources. Many surveys and questionnaires are included in the "working papers."

220. Stough, Ada Barnett. *Brighter vistas: The story of four church programs for older adults.* Washington, D.C.: U.S. Dept. of H.E.W., 1965.

One of a series of case studies published under the overall title of "Patterns for Progress in Aging." The four programs described were those of Protestant churches in Los Angeles, New York, Oklahoma City, and Baton Rouge. The purpose of telling their story was to suggest to other church groups and organizations some of the ways in which they might serve older Americans.

221. Strain, Sister Rose Mary. Retirement among priests and religious. In Bier, William C. (Ed.), *Aging: Its challenge to the individual and society,* Pastoral psychology series (8). New York: Fordham University Press, 1974, 145-63.

Priests and religious must be ready to face retirement too, although the idea is a recent one and did not surface in the church until after Vatican II. Distinguishing one's vocation from one's professional work within that vocation, the writer sees retirement as affecting only the professional work role. Retirement pension plans for priests date only from the 1960s in the U.S. Information is given on the practice in various dioceses. Discussion of problems facing religious communities and their aged members such as social security and the psychological problems of no-longer-working. A final section on retirement responsibilities of individual priests and religious urges on them the value of friendship and of play (leisure).

222. Stressman, Roger. The United Methodist Church and the aging: a developmental study. *Dissertation Abstracts International*, September 1980, *41* (3-A), 1238.

This study seeks to trace the development of ministry to the aged, through the years, on the part of the United Methodist Church and its predecessors, the Methodist Church, the Evangelical Church, and the United Brethren in Christ. The development of homes for the aged was studied, mainly through direct contact with all listed homes of the United Methodist Church. Fifty-two local churches responded to an inquiry about their present work with the aged. It was concluded that this type of ministry is now coming into its own, but that there is still need for developing a sound theology and philosophy of life for the older years—not just providing the "three H's" of health, housing, hobbies. (School of Theology at Claremont, 1980.)

223. The Texas Conference of Churches. *The church and the aging.* Austin, Texas: The Texas Conference of Churches, n.d.

A comparatively short statement with these subheadings: The Church Is Elderly, Looking at the Situation of the Aged, Some Analyses Suggestive of the Need for Change.

224. Thompson, John. Senior Catholics in Action. *Catholic Layman* (formerly *Information*), April 1962, 76, 48-53.

There is little text in this profusely illustrated article, which tells how a San Francisco pastor encourages senior citizens to remain active. Father John Carvlin believes that these aging persons "have rights to the spiritual, human, and material resources of the parish as they 'prep for the finals.' " Mention is made of their projects, their club meetings, their spiritual and entertainment programs.

225. Together Magazine, November 1960, Sunset Issue, *4* (11).

This is a 118-page special issue of a monthly magazine published by the Methodist Publishing House in Nashville. Most of this number is devoted to aging, from a religious aspect.

226. Union of American Hebrew Congregations. *Judaism, the Synagogue, and the aging.* New York: Union of American Hebrew Congregations, 1962.

A sabbath study session (May 1962) sponsored by the UAHC Committee on Aging to "orient members of the Board of Trustees into the complexities of the problem, and to begin the process of crystalizing Reform Jewish thinking about the religious needs of the aging." These *Proceedings* present fourteen notable papers of the said study session, the first two being about "religious foundations."

227. Unitarian Universalist Organization.   *Living all our years.* Boston: Unitarian Universalist Organization, 1965.

Problems of the aged and the ways in which Unitarian societies can serve their aging members. Stress is laid on the need for a philosophy, the need for a plan, and the importance of the minister's attitude. Another section of the document deals with housing for the elderly, and a final summing up suggests ways in which various groups within the church can cooperate.

228. United Presbyterian Church in the USA.   *The church and aging: A survey report of ministries of the United Presbyterian Church in the USA.* New York: United Presbyterian Church, 1967.

This report summarizes a survey that has been made to determine the nature of the United Presbyterian response to the needs of the aged. Significant findings are given and recommendations are made on the following: broad aspects of an approach to ministry for the aging, planning the ministry for the aging, local churches and communities, legislation and pensions, homes for the aging and nursing homes. There are appendices on the research background, on important legislation, on the UPCUSA Board of Pensions; there are also selected data on programs and services for the aging provided by the United Presbyterian Churches.

229. United Presbyterian Church in the USA.   *Manual and directory of United Presbyterian-related health, education, and welfare services.* New York: United Presbyterian Health, Education, and Welfare Association, 1970.

Section 1 is a ready-reference file giving names, locations, and programs provided by more than 400 Presbyterian-related services. Section 2, the manual, outlines standards and recommended procedures with regard to aging (pp. 270-74) and other categories such as hospitals, children's services, neighborhood centers, etc. Section 3 is a detailed directory of Presbyterian agencies by name, location, purpose, etc. (Aging services, A-301 to A-337.) Section 4 contains bibliography, publications, position papers.

230. United Presbyterian Church in the USA.   *The rights and responsibilities of older persons.* Lancaster, Pa.: Program Agency of UPCUSA and the Board of Christian Education of the Presbyterian Church in the USA, October 1973.

Policy statement and recommendations adopted by the 185th General Assembly of the UPCUSA. It addresses these issues: (a) penalizing survival, (b) cultural factors and community attitudes, (c) basis for Christian concern and action, (d) the elderly as a source of strength for society as a whole, (e) major areas of needed response by the church, (f) rights and responsibilities of the elderly. Ten specific recommendations are made.

231. U.S. Catholic Bishops.   *Society and the aged: Toward reconciliation.* Statement issued May 5, 1976.

(Citation 231 continued)
Subheadings: The Aged, Human Rights and the Elderly, The Role of the Church (as individuals, as families, as a community, as advocates of public policy), Towards Reconciliation and "Life to the Full."

232. Vincentian work with the aged. *Catholic Charities Review,* November 1960, *44* (9), 31-32.

In the Detroit Catholic Charities' Department of Aging, numerous requests for diversified services are received from aged persons living alone in their own homes. Parish conferences of the St. Vincent de Paul Society are supplying this kind of service: helping with chores, taking the elderly to church, etc.

233. Wahlstrom, Catherine Lee. Religion and the aged. In Johnson, F. Ernest (Ed.), *Religion and social work.* New York: Harper Bros., 1956.

Care and protection of older people are stressed by the Hebrew and the Christian religions. Catholics have the St. Vincent de Paul Society and the Little Sisters of the Poor; Protestants have institutions and conferences on aging. There are homes for the aged, group programs, services to individuals, community planning. Religion has made a significant contribution to older people. However, many churches are unaware of, or indifferent to, programs for the aging. Much remains to be done.

234. Walker, Gladys H. For the older folks of Bridgeport Diocese: St. Joseph's Manor, Trumbull, Connecticut. *Catholic Digest,* June 1964, *28,* 61-63.

Built by the Catholic diocese of Bridgeport, St. Joseph's Manor houses 285 residents, all over the age of 65, in all stages of health. There are special suites for married couples. One section of the home is for elderly persons who are completely self-sufficient; one section is for those who need some nursing care; a third section accommodates patients who are bedridden. The home is staffed by 20 nuns of the Carmelite order, plus 160 lay employees and teen-age volunteers who call themselves Carmelettes. Driving force behind this model home is Mother Mary Bernadette de Lourdes, member of the 1961 White House Conference on Aging.

235. Weisman, Celia B. *The future is now. A manual for older adult programs in Jewish Communal Service Agencies.* New York: National Jewish Welfare Board, 1976.

A compilation of programs and program resources for the purpose indicated by the title. Part 1, "Defining the Challenge," lays the foundation for program development and includes a typology of aging (intact, moderately impaired, vulnerable). Part 2, "Differential Programming," gives guidelines for program development, with three program classifications meant to match the needs of the three population types identified in part 1.

236. What a parish study reveals: St. Rose of Lima Parish, Milwaukee. *Catholic Charities Review*, December 1959, *43*, 2-3.

The aging in St. Rose of Lima Parish, Milwaukee, participate actively in parish entertainments and reunions. This makes them conscious of their place in the parish and of the interest which the parish has in them.

237. Wheelock, Robert D. The church's response to the elderly: Strategies and opportunities. In Morgan, John H., *Ministering to the elderly: Perspectives and opportunities*. Wichita, Kans.: Institute on Ministry and the Elderly, 1977, 34-44.

Wheelock's remarks are built around these sections: Who are the elderly?, Ministry: A definition, Why minister to the elderly?, What needs to be done to minister to the elderly?, How does a parish respond to the needs of the elderly? The writer believes the opportunities for a congregation to respond are in fact unlimited and that the purpose of his paper was merely "to jog ideas and the tremendous store of creative thoughts that are in your minds." Since the paper was addressed to an audience who had spent three weeks in workshops on the subject, it may not work quite so well for those who merely read the essay.

238. Zenns, William C. A senior citizen day care center. *Catholic Charities Review*, May 1960, *44*, 10-12.

The day-care center described in this article was set up for older people by St. Boniface Parish in downtown Buffalo. It was the outcome of a study conducted by the National Conference on Catholic Charities and by Catholic Charities of Buffalo in 1956, researching the problems and the attitudes of 262 older parishioners. Findings showed great strengths among the aged and a deep desire to remain independent. Replies to a questionnaire showed that they wanted social and recreational activities.

239. Zoot, Vicki A. A program to reduce spiritual deprivation in the nursing home. In Thorson, James A., & Cook, Thomas C., Jr. (Eds.), *Spiritual well-being of the elderly*. Springfield, Ill.: Charles C. Thomas, 1980, 195-97.

The nursing home was in Skokie, Illinois—113 beds, half of them occupied by Jewish residents. A Jewish congregation began a program of weekly services and holiday celebrations in 1976. Religious congregations can be effective in bringing about a positive change in long-term care.

III. SPIRITUAL MINISTRATION TO THE ELDERLY

240. Adkins, Paul Russell. *A study of ministry to the aging through Southern Baptist churches.* Dissertation, New Orleans Baptist Theological Seminary, 1971.

A ministries questionnaire, reproduced in the appendices, was sent to six selected Baptist associations in Florida, South Carolina, New Mexico, Georgia, and Kentucky. Personal interviews were also conducted with directors of 24 Baptist-operated homes for the aged. The problem, as stated in the fourth chapter is, "The senior citizen often loses interest or desire in church activities." The motivation cycle is next explained as a key factor (chapter 5); and the following chapter (chapter 6) looks at "the senior citizen in the light of the motivation cycle." The seventh and final chapter is entitled "Conclusions"; the practical suggestions offered from page 92 to 100 have considerable value and are probably the best part of the dissertation. "Suggestions for Further Research" are made on pages 100-102. Appendices five through ten reproduce the "Mission Ministries Questionnaires," used to gather data; Appendix XI contains the outlines of six workshops. The bibliography contains such references as *Newsweek* and *Webster's Dictionary*, as well as two Greek lexicons.

241. Albers, Thomas L. The Priest and the Aged. *Nuntius Aulae*, 1963, 45, 189-199.

This article is intended primarily for the priest-reader. It is not enough that he be concerned: he needs a sympathetic understanding of the problems of the aged—anxieties and needs common to most old people. He must also see the positive side, that old age is a special time of spiritual enrichment and of child-like joy. A few practical ideas are offered about how a parish might help the aged within its boundaries, but in the reviewer's opinion this last section is rather weak.

242. Allix, Robert. Spirituality and apostolate of old people: the movement, La Vie Montante. *Christ to the World*, 1971, 16 (5), 371-76.

"La Vie Montante" is a movement for persons "of the third age." Begun for the over-60 age bracket by lay people in France during the 1950s, this movement relied on its magazine (circulation 100,000 by 1971), on its mass meetings, and on its team meetings to achieve its goals. Stated aims of the movement are the sanctification of its members and their spiritual and apostolic mobilization for the salvation of the world.

243. Armstrong, Robert, & Armstrong, Priscilla. The church's ministry to older people. *Pulpit Digest*, April 1967, 47 (342), 10-13.

Dilemmas posed by retirement are not only economic, but also moral and spiritual. Our tradition has placed a high value on work and independence. After retirement, in a life of nonwork, a person has to re-evaluate himself. At a later stage, dependency poses a problem. A pastor may refer his older members to appropriate government agencies in order to deal with financial, housing, or medical problems. But he cannot avoid the moral and spiritual questions which come up in the lives of older persons.

244. Bashford, Anthony. First aid in counselling, III: The care of the aged. *Expository Times,* January 1966, *77,* 104-08.

Outlines the major mental disorders of older people as background information for those who minister to the aged. There is, on page 108, a summary of the eight positive attitudes recommended to counsellors. Isolation, infirmity, and retirement are three contributing factors in precipitating mental disturbances in the elderly.

245. Becker, Arthur H. Judgment and grace in the aging process. *Pastoral Psychology,* 1979, *27* (3), 181-90.

Judgment in aging is experienced as the judgment of time: There is little time left to complete projects or to amend what was not well done. For elders, guilt takes the form of fear of rejection and ultimate despair. Pastoral care must strengthen hope, acceptance, and forgiveness. These are very important in ministry to the elderly.

246. Bently, Virgil. *The beauty of age.* Dallas: Gospel Teachers Publications, 1975.

Themes on aging for young and old. Most chapters in this book were originally written as sermons by the author, a Church of Christ minister. Scriptural index and annotated bibliography are provided.

247. Botz, Paschal. Blessed old age. *Worship,* May 1960, *34,* 309-20.

Christian attitudes toward the aged, with citations from the Bible. Old age is seen as a blessing, not a calamity. It is reverenced for its wisdom, experience, and accomplishments.

248. Botz, Paschal. Spiritual aspects of care for the aged. *Hospital Progress,* June 1960, *40,* 63-65.

Attitudes toward the aged: materialistic vs. Christian. Scriptural sayings and models. Seeing Christ in them. Words of Pope Pius XII concerning the aged. Spiritual care of old people: (a) all possible spiritual means to give them strength, (b) their prayers and sufferings have value, (c) helping them face death, (d) eliciting faith and charity by the gift of oneself.

249. Brink, T. L. Pastoral care for the aged: A practical guide. *Journal of Pastoral Care,* 1977, *31* (4), 264-72.

Contents: mental health in later life—crises of aging, like retirement,

changing family relationships, and accumulation of chronic physical condi-
tions; psychopathology, with comments on hypochondria, rigidity of per-
sonality, depression, paranoia, senility, institutional neurosis. Treatment for
the elderly – define the scope of fruitful intervention; direct your remarks to
the elder; objectively take a history; identify problems; solve problems
directly; resolve guilt complexes; provide opportunities for socialization and
emotional support.

250. Brown, J. Paul. *Counseling with senior citizens.* Englewood Cliffs:
Prentice Hall, 1964.

From the foreword: "J. Paul Brown has skillfully interpreted the various
factors associated with the aging process, and the role of the church in deal-
ing with . . . elderly men and women." There are chapters on: "The Role of
Religion in the Aging Process," "The Three Generation Family," "Selecting a
Senior Citizens Home," "Emotional Factors in Aging," "Marital Problems of
Senior Citizens," "Financing the Senior Years," "The Senior Citizen Helps
Himself."

251. Butler, Clarence. Pastoral needs of older persons: A clinical
approach. *Journal of Pastoral Care,* 1968, 22 (2), 75-81.

Describes, from a clinical point of view, how one family adjusted to the
problem of advanced age and retirement. A pastor has a duty to help *all* of
his congregation to integrate themselves and to accommodate changes into
a new continuity. Warns to be aware of any extreme changes in the retiree's
life – psychological, sociological, or theological.

252. Buxbaum, Robert E. Use of religious resources in the care of the
aged. *Journal of Religion and Health,* April 1969, 8, 143-62.

Failure to utilize distinctively religious resources deprives the patient of the
most creative, valuable, and meaningful ones available. The writer, a
Presbyterian minister with long experience as a chaplain in the San Antonio
State Hospital, is now a professional counsellor. His article, originally a
paper delivered at the Southwest Methodist Jurisdiction Conference on the
Aging (1968) is strong in its psychological background.

253. Cale, W. Franklin. What I expect from my church. *Mature Living,*
June 1980, 4 (9), 16.

An elderly person speaks out plainly on what he thinks he has a right to
expect from his church: that the church's attitude will not be only, "What
can we do for these old folks?" The church should minister *with* the elderly
and not fall victim to the youth syndrome.

254. Caligiuri, Angelo M. Aging and the Spiritual Life. *Spiritual Life,*
Spring 1979, 25, 41-46.

(Citation 254 continued)

At the outset of the article, the author declares that it is his intent to reflect on "the reality of the spiritual life as it is present in the lives of all who believe, and as it is being lived by all the followers of Christ now, and then offer some observations about that same life as it is lived and expressed in that period of life which we call aging." In fact, general reflections on spirituality and the spiritual life occupy the major portion of his article. Only about one page is explicitly devoted to "spirituality and aging."

255. Campbell, Oscar P. Organizing older adults in the church. *International Journal of Religious Education*, Oct. 1953, *30*, 6-7.

Suggests a survey should be conducted locally, listing all older adults, with special reference to their needs, interests, talents, skills, and how they spend their leisure time. The homebound should be visited by younger people or by active older adults. The church should provide personal counselling, such as on making wills, arranging for pensions, insurance, social security benefits. Finally, the church must remember that persons need to develop spiritually as long as they live and must provide these persons with opportunities for study and service to others.

256. Carlson, Paul. Ministry to the elderly. *Ministries*, July 1980, *1* (6), 25; 33.

Ministry to the aged confined in their homes is especially suited for Catholic permanent deacons. Examples are given.

257. Carmelettes serve the aging. *Catholic Charities Review*, 1967, *51* (6), 9-11.

"Carmelettes" are young women volunteers who, in a variety of ways, assist in residences for the aging operated by the Carmelite Order of nuns. Presented are some excerpts illustrative of the kinds of services which it is possible for young people to offer in such homes.

258. Castellan, F. H. W. Apostolate of old people in Japan. *Christ to the World*, 1972, *17* (1), 42-46.

Institutions for the aged offer missionaries a magnificent field for the apostolate. This missionary priest, accompanied by a Japanese Sister and a lay volunteer, visits the elderly and finds a receptive audience.

259. Clements, William M. (Ed.) *Ministry with the aging: Designs, challenges, foundations.* San Francisco: Harper & Row, 1981.

This book combines in one impressive volume the contributions of 16 scholars well qualified in the field of religion and aging. Chapter titles and their authors are as follows: "Introduction: The New Context for Ministry with the Aging" by William M. Clements; "Age and Aging in the Old Testament" by Rolf Knierim; "The Elderly in the Life and Thought of the Early

Church" by Jean Laporte; "Cultural Antecedents to Contemporary American Attitudes toward Aging" by Martin E. Marty; "Christian Theology and Aging: Basic Affirmations" by Martin Heinecken; "Worship and Aging: Memory and Repentance" by Urban T. Holmes; "Aging: On the Way to One's End" by Ann Belford Ulanov; "Retirement" by Evelyn Eaton Whitehead and James D. Whitehead; "Ethical Aspects of Aging in America" by John C. Bennett; "Religion and the Elderly in Today's World" by Barbara Payne; "The Family Relations of Older Persons" by Allen Moore; "Adults with Parents in Crisis: A Personal Account" by James W. Ewing; "Education for Ministry with the Aging" by Melvin A. Kimble; "Death, Dying, and the Elderly" by George Paterson; "Adult Religious Education and the Aging" by Donald E. Miller; "Lay Ministeries with Older Adults" by Elbert C. Cole.

260. Clingan, Donald F. *Aging persons in the community of faith.* Indianapolis: The Indiana Commission on the Aging and the Aged, for the Institute on Religion and Aging, 1975.

Subtitled "A congregational guidebook for churches and synagogues on ministry to, for, and with the aging," this is a "revised and updated version of *The Older Person, the Church, and the Community,* by Walter H. Moeller." Contents are chapters on: "The Needs of the Aging"; "How Does a Congregation Begin Ministry with the Aging?"; "The Call of the Clergy and Lay Leaders to Involvement"; "The Unique Role of Congregations in Ministry with the Aging"; "Congregations and Communities Moving Together in Ministry with the Aging"; "A New Commitment." [NB: The writer, Clingan, was a delegate to the 1971 White House Conference on Aging and first president of the National Interfaith Coalition on Aging.]

261. Cook, Thomas C., Jr., & McGinty, Donna L. *So even to old age.* Athens, Ga.: National Interfaith Coalition on Aging, 1977.

National religious and secular leadership assessed current gerontological training and future needs in the linking of religious and secular educational systems, with a view to enhancing the spiritual well-being of older persons. This is a final report on the assessment. Appendix B reports on the National Intra-decade Conference on the Spiritual Well-Being of the Elderly, held at Atlanta in April of 1977. Appendix C supplies an abstract of a training project in aging education for seminary faculties and the clergy at large.

262. Davis, David C. A Pastoral Ministry to Older Persons. *AMHC Forum,* 1975, *27* (3), 103-05.

The initials in the title of this publication stand for Association of Mental Health Clergy, Inc. (400 Forest Avenue, Buffalo, New York 14213). The first half of the short feature article here reviewed is composed of commonplaces in the literature: people today are living longer, the percentage of older people in the population is greater, Western culture emphasizes youth. Frequently cited Bible quotations are repeated. The second half of the article deals with four main areas of concern which older people experience: loss of self-esteem, increased significance of death, more meaningful religion, and a re-living of the past. Senility poses the greatest barrier in working with older persons. Suggestions are made for churches, ways in which a group of older persons felt that the church could make it easier for them to be part of the congregation.

263. Deneen, Sister Francis Mary. The word of God speaks to the elderly. *The Bible Today*, February 1975, *13* (76), 266-71.

Forty-one brief passages from the Scriptures, arranged in such a way as to convey a message to the aged.

264. Dortzbach, Elmer. The role of the clergy in the life of the aged. *Dissertation Abstracts International*, May 1976, *36* (11-A), 7673.

To test the validity of ministers' training for work with the aged, two matched questionnaires were employed. One was administered to selected seminary academic deans, and the other to selected Denver-area clergymen. Findings indicated that the clergymen were dissatisfied with their preparation in gerontology; the seminaries planned some improvement in training, but less than the clergy desired. The clergymen's actual relationship with the aged was adjudged satisfactory, though some areas were in need of improvement. (University of Colorado, 1975.)

265. Drapela, Victor J. In-service training for pastoral counselors. *Journal of Religion and Health*, 1974, *13* (2), 142-46.

Practical suggestions on how to provide training opportunities for clergymen involved in practical ministry. Deals with the locale, the time, and structuring of in-service meetings. There is a report on one such in-service workshop in the Tampa Bay area. One brief paragraph on page 145 deals with "understanding the aged."

266. Dunn, Patricia, & Helminiak, Daniel A. Spiritual Practices for the Elderly. *Spirituality Today*, June 1981, *33*, 122-36.

"This presentation summarizes our tested conclusions about spiritual practices for the elderly." Varieties of prayer are discussed at length, from the viewpoint of how they might prove practical for the elderly. Specific spiritual practices are advised to meet the several kinds of loneliness described. The ability to accept pain and to "forgive its cause" is also a goal of ministry to the elderly. The issue of approaching death, it is suggested, might be brought up as a topic for discussion; the elderly might write up their own obituary and then discuss it with others, in pairs and as a group.

267. Education for Ministry in Aging: Gerontology in Seminary Training. *Theological Education*, Winter 1980, *16* (3), special issue.

(Citation 267 continued)

This special issue, the pagination of which runs from page 271 to page 414, contains four main parts: Part I is on "Aging and Theological Education" by David O. Moberg. Part II is on "Education for Ministry in Aging: Guidelines for Contemporary Objectives" and contains (among other things) eight articles on "interdisciplinary approaches and concerns," plus six more on "strategies for using the guidelines." Part III is entitled "Emerging Curricular Models for Education for Ministry in Aging," and has seven articles plus a page (388) of references. Part IV is a single article by Reuel L. Howe on "Bringing Spirit to Aging Education in the '80's."

The appendix lists national consultants to Project-GIST and lists the Project-GIST staff; participants in Project-GIST, 1977-1979; fifty-four abstracts of GIST sub-projects; and finally, a list of organizations and agencies with direct participation or representation in Project-GIST ("Gerontology In Seminary Training").

268. Fahey, Charles J.   Spiritual well-being of the elderly in relation to God. In Thorson, James A., & Cook, Thomas C., Jr. (Eds.), *Spiritual well-being of the elderly.* Springfield, Ill.: Charles C. Thomas, 1980, 61-63.

A quest for holiness is a lifelong task, also for the aged: prayer, moral behavior, love of God and neighbor, and witness. It is the responsibility of the church to help *all* men be free, and so there should be a ministry to the aged as well.

269. Faunce, Frances Avery.   The nursing home visitor: A handbook written from the inside. New York: Abingdon Press, 1969.

Comments are made on the need for visitors, on helping visitors understand the viewpoint of the resident, and what is involved in moving to a nursing home. There are suggestions for the visitor.

270. Ford, Steven R.   The social process of aging: Its implications for pastoral ministry. *Pastoral Psychology,* Spring 1981, 29 (3), 203-15.

If our ministry is to affirm the humanity of older men and women, it is necessary that we cease to look upon them as complexes of typical traits. Healing ministry is possible only when the Christian pastor enters into a genuinely human relationship with the elderly person. This is possible only if America's cultural bias against the aged and the power of social convention is overcome.

271. Fournier, William, OMI and O'Malley, Sarah, OSB.   *Age and grace: Handbook of programs for the ministry to the aging.* Collegeville, Minnesota: The Liturgical Press, 1981.

This handbook contains "methods and models of ministry which have been tried and which work." After what amounts to an introductory chapter ("1. Aging: Journey Towards Fullness"), chapter two gives a two-page "Rationale for Parish Ministry," which the authors feel must be intergenerational and parish-centered. Chapter three, on "Parish Programs: Implementation" briefly discusses such preliminaries as a statistical survey of the parish, nursing home contact, a letter to shut-ins, an introductory parish liturgy, a meeting for volunteers, telephone committee, and in-service programs for those engaged in this ministry. "Possible Areas of Volunteer Involvement" are taken up in chapter four and "Sample Letters, Forms, and Agendas" are offered in chapter five. The book concludes with "Audiovisual Resource Materials," a Bibliography, and "Additional Areas for the Ministry to the Aging" listed on two unnumbered pages at the rear. As a handbook, it is clear and practical; however, there is not much said about any one aspect or phase of the project.

272. Fox, Alfred. Ministers' Workshop: Tapping the resources of time. *Christianity Today*, April 24, 1981, *25*, 52.

"Older members are a reservoir of good will and experience and deserve consultant status in all areas of church life." They are not only a promising source of ministry to every age group, but are also a useful "experience bank." By tapping this potential of the church's older members, pastors can afford them a meaningful role and help others to benefit by their experience.

273. Friendly visiting with older persons. *Catholic Charities Review*, October 1960, *44*, 21-24.

Discusses friendly visiting under church auspices for people who are lonely. Once a week, the gift of one's own person as companion to a selected elderly person. For this purpose, cultivate the resources of the retired themselves, also the St. Vincent de Paul Society. To be a full success, the friendly visiting service should function as one in a network of services which older persons may require.

274. Gariboldi, Ronald John. Caring relationships with the institutionalized elderly as ministry. *Dissertation Abstracts International*, May 1976, *36* (11-A), 7483.

A theological investigation of the work of activity directors in nursing homes, with implications for the official ministry of the church. Focus is on Karl Rahner's analysis of *caritas*, of symbol, and of ministry. Seeks to develop the theological meaning of psychosocial data. Taped interviews with three activity directors.

275. Goodling, Richard A. (Ed.). *The church's ministry to the homebound.* Nashville: The Methodist Church, General Board of Education, 1967.

Resources and guidelines for visitors to the homebound aged. Report of a Methodist-sponsored seminar held in April 1965 and attended by pastors and selected leaders in adult education.

276. Greene, Padraig. The pastoral care of the aged. *Furrow*, February 1979, *30*, 90-94.

Suggests finding what aging means to each individual in order to find out how best that person's needs can be met. One needs time to pray with the old, to have confession and anointing, and give a few words of encouragement. A visit from the priest is a special occasion for them, a chance to empathize and to listen responsively. Parties for the aged, outings, visitation groups must be part and parcel of every parish. Those aged who are able should have the opportunity of attending Mass, transportation being provided by parishioners.

277. Hammond, Phillip E. Aging and the ministry. In Riley, Matilda White; Riley, John W., Jr.; & Johnson, Marilyn E. (Eds.). *Aging and society: Aging and the professions.* (Vol. 2.) New York: Russell Sage Foundation, 1969, 293-323.

An examination of the part played by the church and by church-sponsored activities in the life of the aged parishioner. Though many programs exist, the author argues that there is no clear theoretical base for their evaluation. This leads him to discuss church strategy for ministering to the needs of old people. Concerns and opportunities presented to the church today are identified and discussed.

278. Harris, Thomas A. Toward a ministry to the aging and the elderly, the forgotten and neglected. *Dissertation Abstracts International*, April 1979, *39* (10-A), 6183.

The message is that opportunities must be provided for older persons to find meaning, activity, and fulfillment in the fellowship of the church. This essay looks at needs and problems of the elderly and offers proposals and plans for implementation.

279. Hougland, Kenneth. Liberation from age-ism: The ministry of elders. *Christian Century*, 27 March 1974, *91*, 340-42.

The ministry of the elderly is to use their wisdom and their abilities in the service of others. To do this, they will have to break out of the "no longer needed role" to which society has assigned them. The services which they might perform are limitless. "No one should die before his life is over."

280. John XXIII, Pope. Gemmarum instar. *Acta Apostolicae Sedis*, September 1961, *53*, 605-06.

Latin text: "Our Lady of Consolation" is declared the heavenly patroness of the aged in Italy. The date is May 26, 1961.

281. John XXIII, Pope. Allocutio in anniversario coronationis. *Acta Apostolicae Sedis*, December 1961, *53*, 760-70.

"Longevity is a gift from God." Italian text of an allocution given on November 4, 1961, when he himself turned 80.

282. Jungkuntz, Daniel; Krawinkel, Robert; & Siegel, Lawrence.
Spiritual aspects. In Cowdry, Edmund V., & Steinbert, Franz U. (Eds.)
The care of the geriatric patient (4th ed.). St. Louis: C. V. Mosby, 1971,
411-16.

The 32nd chapter contains three "viewpoints" on religious pastoral care of
the elderly: (a) "A Jewish Point of View" by Rabbi Lawrence Siegel. Valuable
information for those dealing with elderly Jewish patients—cultural attitudes, kosher food, things they might appreciate; (b) "A Catholic Point of
View" by Father Robert Krawinkel. Subheadings: Meaning of Life, Meaning
of Suffering, Meaning of Death, Confession, Holy Communion, Sacrament
of the Sick; (c) "A Protestant Point of View" by Rev. Daniel Jungkuntz [no
denomination given]. Subheadings: Confronting Reality as a Geriatric
Patient, Discovering the Goodness of God as a Geriatric Patient, Spiritual
Growth in the Geriatric Patient.

283. Keith, Pat M.   Perceptions of needs of aged by ministers and elderly.
Review of Religious Research, 1977, *18*, 278-82.

Private interviews with 50 men and 74 women, all 65 and over, who were
randomly selected. Twenty-four out of 30 ministers in the same city completed a questionnaire. All, ministers as well as elderly, were asked to
evaluate the need for additional services in 23 health and social service
categories. Data showed significant agreement; but the ministers assigned
church relationships the fourth priority, while the elderly ranked these relationships fifteenth. The focus of the elderly was primarily on supportive services rather than on participation in organized community activities.

284. Kerr, Horace.   *How to minister to senior adults in your church.*
Nashville: Broadman Press, 1980.

This book combines the *what* and the *why* with a practical, step-by-step
guide for developing a ministry with older persons in the church. Parts of the
book are: (a) A Rationale for Ministry, (b) Planning for Ministry, (c) Providing a Balanced Program, (d) Enlarging Your Vision.

285. Kilduff, Thomas.   Aging. *Spiritual Life*, Spring 1980, *26*, 3-20.

This article "is the text of two talks delivered at the Summer Workshop on
Retirement at Catholic University in July, 1979." The first part is a theology
of aging, which seeks to find the meaning of the aging process in the light of
faith. The second part deals with the spirituality of the aging person or the
subjective living of these objective theological realities. Theology sees aging
as a call; spirituality considers one's personal response to it. "Our theology
suggests that the losses of aging and experienced dependence in the later
years must be turned into gain in creative leisure and happy presence to
Christ and others."

286. King, J. Carter III.   First Southern Presbyterian Church – One look at ministry with aging people. *Austin Seminary Bulletin* (Faculty ed.), Oct. 1980, 96 (3), 31-38.

This case study attempts to trace some of a church's more recent efforts at ministry with aging people. The church is a downtown, 600-member congregation in Austin, and the new directions described began in 1974. A task force was made responsible for pastoral care and Bible studies by the pastoral staff, the Sunday morning worship service tape program, the shut-in adoption program, and "Senior Tuesdays."

287. Knapp, Kenneth R.   Respect for age in Christianity: The base of our concern in Scripture and tradition. *Social Thought*, Spring 1976, 2 (2), 9-21.

The title aptly summarizes the thrust of this article. The bulk of it is devoted to Scriptural sources, though some secondary sources are also identified in Christian history.

288. Knoy, Zane, & Johnson, Richard.   *A bibliography on ministry and aging.* Durham, N. H.: New England Gerontology Center, n.d., Mimeo.

Pages 2 to 26 simply reprint, with no changes, the annotated bibliography published in 1976 by the National Interfaith Coalition on Aging. Pages 28 to 31 list 24 items under the heading, Material Available on Ministry of the Church to Older Persons. This material consists largely of pamphlets issued by various denominations.

289. Kragnes, Earl N.   Insights for the later years. *Christian Century*, May 13, 1981, 98, 533-34.

What model could be used to develop a theology of aging? The author suggests a theology of blessing based on four insights from Bruce C. Birch of Wesley Seminary. These insights are based on "the wisdom tradition, [which] may lead us to some grasp of the meaning of aging and oldness in Western culture."

290. Lampe, M. Willard.   Religious needs of the patient. *Bulletin of the Institute of Gerontology, State Univ. of Iowa*, February 1960, 7 (Suppl. 2), 3-4.

Lessons are drawn on this topic from four elderly persons with whom the writer was dealing and to whose religious needs he ministers. All elderly persons need continued activity.

291. Leport, Father.   [First name not given.] Two parishes renewed by the apostolate of old people. *Christ to the World*, 1971, 16, 294-98.

When elderly people are given suitable guidance, they can help other persons of their own age spiritually, to find faith and the love of God. This article shows how the pastor of two very de-Christianized parishes in Brittany carried on a fruitful apostolate among his elderly parishioners and how he obtained their collaboration in his parish ministry. To do so, he had recourse to the movement known as "La Vie Montante." (See citation 242.)

292. Longino, Charles F., Jr. Parish clergy and the aged: Examining assumptions. *Gerontologist*, 1975, *15* (#5, pt. 2), 68.

Out of a national sample (N = 654) of American Baptist parish clergy who had been asked to rate their satisfaction with 52 ministerial roles, 60% said that they enjoyed ministering to the aged; only 5% definitely did not. Those who derived greater satisfaction from duties with an expressive role orientation were also more likely to find satisfaction in working with the aged.

293. Longino, Charles F., & Kitson, Gay C. Parish clergy and the aged: Examining stereotypes. *Journal of Gerontology*, 1976, *31*, 340-45.

In a similar article to citation 292, using the same data from a national sample of 654 American Baptist parish ministers, the writers reiterate that the majority of the clergy studied do not have an aversion toward ministering to older people. There is, however, some indication of an ageist attitude. It is also found that pastoral calls from clergy and church friends are very important to older persons.

294. Lynch, Philip Arthur. Bible study: a model of ministry with older adults in an institutional setting. *Dissertation Abstracts International*, December 1978, *39* (6-A), 3641.

Individuals moving into a facility for the aging frequently experience problems of adjustment. Religious beliefs, along with certain Bible themes and peer groups support, can assist in the process of adjusting. The project described in this dissertation was a Bible study group organized in a facility for the aging. Each member was first interviewed to assess individual needs, then twelve sessions were held on different themes selected by group members. After the twelve sessions, each group member was again interviewed. Results of the survey indicated a general trend of positive growth and adjusting. (Lancaster Theological Seminary, 1978.)

295. McClellan, Robert W. *Claiming a frontier: Ministry and older people.* Los Angeles: University of Southern California, Ethel P. Andrus Gerontology Center, 1977.

Written by a Presbyterian pastor with 31 years of broad experience in churches, this Doctor of Ministry dissertation aims at evaluating techniques for revitalizing church ministry to the aged. Includes sample models of programs used by various religious centers around the country. Chapter six "offers specific guidelines, to enable leaders to work at the grass roots in developing and evaluating ministries to older people."

296. McKeon, Richard M. The clergy and the aging. *Pastoral Life*, May-June 1960, 8 (3), 30-35.

(Citation 296 continued)

This article amplifies some of the suggestions made at the New York Governor's Conference on the Aging in 1955, in its section on "the role of religion." Headings: Limited Time for Salvation, Problem of Feeling Rejected, Visit the Aged, Special Catholic Action, Leisure Time for Spiritual Development, What Can Be Done within the Parish.

297. McNally, Arthur. Everyone has a harvest time: Facing the prospect of old age as Christ faced the Passion. *Sign*, February 1963, *42*, 52-53.

One's attitude toward growing old can be the same as that of Christ toward His Passion: the climax of life, the final fulfillment of a mission on earth.

298. Manno, Bruno V. The church and older people: A training program. *Religious Education*, November-December 1978, *73*, 699-706.

This is a report on a program, originally Roman Catholic, but also used by several Protestant churches, training lay people to administer to the needs of the elderly. The program is described in detail, and an evaluation is included.

299. Marino, Robert, & Sidney, Walter. Communal anointing of the elderly. *Modern Liturgy*, April 1978, *5*, 24-25.

Argues that sickness or old age is primarily an experience of separation and fragmentation. The rite of anointing seeks to heal this isolation by affirming the value of these people within the community and thus restoring to them a sense of wholeness.

300. Maves, Paul B. *Older people and the church.* New York: Abingdon-Cokesbury Press, 1949.

This book was (according to the foreword) "the first comprehensive attempt to study the relationship of Protestant churches to people over sixty years of age. . . . Its purpose is to serve as an inclusive book of background material and concrete action suggestions for church leaders concerned with the ministry of the church to those in later maturity." There are four parts: (a) Aging and the Church, (b) Pastoral Care of Older People, (c) Group Work with Older People, (d) Social Resources and the Church.

301. Maves, Paul B. Pastoral work with older people. *Pastoral Psychology*, 1950, *1* (2), 42-48.

A popularly written article, which aims at persuading ministers to call on elderly people. It is good, but not particularly informative, as it is not a research-type article with data-based insights. There are a few concrete suggestions such as using older lay assistants to help with the visiting.

302. Methodist Church Board of Education. *The Church's ministry to the homebound: Resources and guidelines for visitors to the homebound aged.* Nashville: General Board of Education of the Methodist Church — Division of the Local Church, 1965, Mimeo.

(Citation 302 continued)

The report of a seminar held in Durham, N.C., April 25-30, 1965, cosponsored by the Divinity School of Duke University and the Methodist "Division of the Local Church" as indicated above. The main divisions of the report are: The Aged Homebound, Personal and Social Needs, Services Available to the Aged and Their Families, Visitation Procedure and Findings.

303. Mills, Beatrice Marie. The educational interests and needs of older adults in selected Presbyterian churches. *Dissertation Abstracts,* January 1969, *29* (7-A), 2086.

The sample consisted of 8 ministers and 187 adult resident members 65 years of age and over (63 men and 124 women) in 8 churches within the Presbytery of Indianapolis. Specific interests or needs indicated by at least 13% of the older adults included Bible study, motion pictures in church, group singing, discussion groups. Methods used by the ministers to identify needs and interests of the elderly were limited to personal inquiry and general observation; 41% of the ministers used no method at all. (University of Indiana, 1968.)

304. Ministries in aging: A survey report on planned church programs for older persons in New Mexico. Santa Fe, N. M.: n.p., 1965.

In addition to already existing institutional ministries to the older persons living in retirement facilities, hospitals, and nursing homes, there is the emergence of social ministries to the aging in many communities. Of special interest: "Church Programs in Aging: Ministries to the Aged in New Mexico"; "Availability of Church Equipment and Facilities for Social Activities"; "Churches Reporting Opportunities for Older Members to Serve as Volunteers"; and "Reporting Ministries to the Aging."

305. Moberg, David O. Aging and its implications for theological education. *Journal of Pastoral Care,* June 1970, *24,* 127-34.

Theological education, understood as preparation for church leadership in the role of priest, minister, or rabbi, must include specific attention to the aging. Motives include (among others mentioned) the current needs and numbers of the aged; their neglect, even by the helping professions. Methods include workshops and seminars, planning courses into seminary curricula, clinical pastoral training in homes for the aged.

306. Moberg, David O. Needs felt by the clergy for ministries to the aging. *Gerontologist,* 1975, *15* (2), 70-175.

A survey of 109 clergymen in 11 ministerial associations of the Greater Milwaukee area revealed that only 29% of them had had any formal training in ministering to the old. As a result, a one-day workshop was held, centering on spiritual well-being. The usefulness of such surveys and workshops is suggested for parish clergy.

307. Moberg, Richard Gordon. The attitudes of ministers toward old people. *Dissertation Abstracts International,* December 1969, *30* (6-A), 2619.

Sixty parish ministers of the United Church of Christ were matched for education with a group of 60 Rotarians to compare their attitudes towards old people. The finding was that ministers evaluated old people as negatively as did nonministers.

308. Monk, Abraham, & Cryns, Arthur G. Predictors of voluntaristic intent among the aged. *Gerontologist,* 1974, *14* (#5, pt. 1), 425-29.

This bit of research studied the correlation between stated interest in community volunteer work and a number of variables characterizing aged individuals in a white, working-class ethnic neighborhood of Buffalo. Six such variables were identified as age, education, belief in one's ability to serve, interest in senior citizen activity, scope of special interests, home ownership. The correlation of *age* with "voluntaristic intent" was found to be both significant and negative.

309. Montgomery, J. Dexter. *The Church's ministry to older persons: A manual for church leaders.* Indianapolis: The United Christian Missionary Society (1956?).

The purpose of this popularly written manual is to offer guidance to church leaders in planning their ministry to older persons. Fifteen short chapters include background information about "older adults," planning the program, discovering resources, discovering and training leaders. A list gives addresses for the nine homes for older persons then supported by the National Benevolent Association of Christian Churches (Disciples of Christ), the body that authorized this booklet.

310. Morgan, John H. *Ministering to the elderly: Perspectives and opportunities.* Wichita, Kans.: Institute on Ministry and the Elderly, 1977.

This small book contains a brief foreword by Seward Hiltner and three essays edited by the Reverend John H. Morgan, director of the aforesaid institute. The essays are: "The Older American: Social Psychological Needs," by Helen Znaniecki Lopata; "Ministering to the Elderly: Needs, Perspectives, and Opportunities," by William B. Oglesby, Jr.; "The Church's Response to the Elderly: Strategies and Opportunities," by Robert D. Wheelock. Included is a select bibliography of only 16 titles and short biographical notes on the editor and contributors.

311. Murphy, Sister Patricia. *Healing with time and love: A guide for visiting the elderly.* Los Angeles: University of Southern California, Ethel P. Andrus Gerontology Center, 1979.

Contents: "Introduction," "You Are Your Best Gift," "The Convalescent Home," "The Elderly Resident," "The Visitor."

76

312. Nouwen, Henri J. M.; Naus, Peter; & McNeill, Don. Aging and ministry. *Journal of Pastoral Care*, September 1974, *28* (3), 164-82.

Part 1, "Aging": "Introduction," "Aging as a Way to Darkness" (segregation, desolation, loss of self), "Aging as a Way to Light" (hope, humor, vision).

Part 2, "Aging and Ministry": "The Aging Minister" (poverty, compassion), "Ministry to the Aging" (ministry of acceptance, of confrontation).

313. Novick, Louis J. The role of the Rabbi in an orthodox long-term geriatric hospital. *Journal of Jewish Communal Service*, 1975, *51* (4), 373-80.

After describing the needs of long-term patients and explaining some beliefs and practices of orthodox Judaism, the author depicts the rabbi's role as he understands it. He stresses the need of being recognized as a departmental head in the facility, as well as the importance of the rabbi's cooperating with other departmental heads and with the staff in general. The insight which he offers into the world of elderly Jewish residents' religious expectations should prove very helpful to chaplains of other faiths who are in contact with such residents.

314. Oglesby, William B., Jr. Ministering to the elderly: Needs, perspectives, and opportunities. In Morgan, John H., *Ministering to the elderly: Perspectives and opportunities.* Wichita, Kans.: Institute on Ministry and the Elderly, 1977, 21-33.

The author's stated purpose is to set forth factors which he believes essential for ministering to the elderly. They are: 1. a renewed awareness of the inherent worth of persons; 2. the continual process of working through basic relationships; 3. the discovery of meaning at every point in life; and 4. the concept of hope. In the light of these dimensions of an aging ministry, three pages are then presented on the relationship between pastor and parishioner and on the broader perspective of minister/congregation.

315. Payne, Barbara. Pain denial and ministry to the elderly. *Theology Today*, April 1968, *38*, 30-36.

The role of religion in responding to pain and to dying is a neglected area of research, says the author. She reports on an exploratory study of the spiritual dimension of the chronic illness and the dying of the elderly. Specifically, she examines the religious responses of 40 elderly patients, 10 hospice workers, and 10 pastors in Atlanta to dying and to the pain of chronic illness. Patients' ages ranged from 64 to 94, with more than 50% being between the ages of 64 and 74; the number of males and females observed was equal. On the part of workers and pastors, the most frequent response to the pain of the elderly was to listen sympathetically, to discuss it with the person, to pray and meditate, to talk about everything and anything as a distraction. The elderly's response to pain is also reported, and three main types of "implications for ministry" are spelled out.

316. Peacock, Richard L. Older adult: The church's opportunity. *Southwestern Journal of Theology*, Spring 1975, *17*, 48-57.

This article covers: need for ministry to the older adult; planning for ministry to the older adult: statement of purpose, immediate objectives, important ideas in building an effective program, resources, helping the older adult continue to be a productive member of society, pre-retirement planning; ministry to the homebound: their five needs, outreach for lost older adults, motivation for ministry to older adults.

317. Phillips, Ambrose K. The Roman Catholic chaplain in a long-term care facility. *Concern in the Care of the Aging*, Feb.-May 1978, *4* (4-5), 14-19.

Discusses the chaplain's responsibility, in the sense of ability to respond. He must be able to listen in the first place—listen to God and listen to humanity. He must be able to respond to the health-care team, to patients or residents, to families, to staff, to community. His is the responsibility of educating the community and those young people who are entering the field of the ministry.

318. Phillips, Ambrose K. The chaplain's role in a nursing home. *Hospital Progress*, June 1973, *54*, 75-78.

Suggests that the chaplain must help elderly individuals realize that life is a blessing. He helps set the spiritual atmosphere of the entire home. It is important that residents feel they are being ministered to by a particular individual—that the chaplain is "their" priest. Catholic sacramental ministry to the elderly includes the Eucharist, Penance, and the Sacrament of the Sick. All three are commented on with special reference to the elderly.

319. Protestant Episcopal Church. *Experiment in training volunteers: A manual based on the Sargent House project.* Washington, D.C.: Episcopal Diocese of Washington, D.C.: Episcopal Diocese of Washington, 1962.

Experiences of the 1950s in working with the aged led the Diocese of Washington, D.C. (Episcopal) to institute a two-year training program for leaders. Seventy-one percent of the volunteers who completed training at Sargent House were 60 years of age or older at the time of their application; nine of them were in their seventies. Of those who participate in activities at Sargent House, an increasing number have been moving on to the role of a group leader; they enter a training course and become regular "volunteers."

320. Quinn, Philip F., & Talley, Kay. A clergy training program in a mental health center. *Hospital and Community Psychiatry*, 1974, *25*, 472-73.

A Tampa mental health center initiated a six-month pilot program in 1971 to teach counseling skills to clergymen. Participating clergymen exercised their skills in working with the aged and the terminally ill. Lectures on aging were given by an intake worker with a master's degree in gerontology.

321. Rank, Betty Jane. Role of the volunteer in Catholic-sponsored centers and clubs. *Catholic Charities Review*, October 1965, *49*, 8-12.

The growing interest in services to the aging includes recreational and group work. This article points up the need for clubs and centers and for volunteers to work in them. An opportunity exists for churches to help the elderly adjust to life's changes. The qualifications are described for volunteers (as distinct from leaders chosen from among the members themselves). Professionally trained staff is needed if the program is to operate several days a week and is to meet a wide range of needs.

322. Reichert, Sara, & Reichert, Richard. *In wisdom and the Spirit: A religious education program for those over 65.* New York: Paulist Press, 1976.

This volume is divided into three parts: 1. overview of the elderly as they are and how they learn; 2. the five "units" which make up the program, each unit being a separate topic for a catechesis to the elderly (these topics are: a. the phenomenon; b. priesthood of the elderly; c. prayer and the spiritual life; d. reconciliation and the Eucharist; e. death, dying, and the resurrection); 3. some suggested craft projects.

323. Reisch, Harold W. The minister and the elderly. *Pastoral Psychology*, January 1967, *17* (170), 41-48.

To whom does the elderly person turn for help when he faces the adjustments which aging and retirement bring in their wake? For what does he ask? The help that he receives from his minister will be colored by the way the pastor sees the elderly person and by the resources which he knows and uses. The article ends with a listing of voluntary agencies, public agencies, national organizations, and denominational national offices dealing with church-related social welfare.

324. Robb, Thomas Bradley. A study of the social and psychological foundations for ministry with older persons, with suggestions for alternatives to present forms of ministry. *Dissertation Abstracts International*, August 1971, *32* (2-A), 1067.

A study based on the assumption that present programs of ministry with older adults are inadequate because of a lack of understanding on the part of church leaders and the lack of an adequate theory of aging. Part I relates the needs of older persons to the resources of the local church: needs for (1) protective and supportive care; (2) maintenance care; (3) preventive care. The role of the local church is discussed in relation to each type of care and suggestions are made for initiating programs. Part II surveys current literature on aging as a developmental process and concludes that the Cumming-Henry theory of disengagement does not account for the phenomenon of aging, nor describe it as a developmental process. An alternative hypothesis proposed is that aging is a progressive.shifting in the balance between two choices: toward autonomy and toward homonomy, with increasing emphasis on the latter with advancing age. (Graduate Theological Union, 1970.)

325. Rost, Robert Anthony. A holistic method of parish ministry with older people. *Dissertation Abstracts International,* July 1980, *41* (1-A), 0290.

Describes a project in ministry with older people based on two years' experience at St. Augustine's Catholic Parish in Kansas City, Missouri. About one-fifth of the parish were over 60 years of age. Adaptation is difficult for the elderly because of their resistance to change, the breakdown of support systems, limited finances and mobility, and their own vulnerability to crime. For many older people, the parish provides some kind of continuity and stability. An "Adult Social Club" was formed to provide opportunities for socializing and occasional service activities. On the whole, their strength seems to lie in their faith, their independence, their interpersonal bonds. (Catholic University of America, 1979.)

326. Rowe, Gard Linwood. Establishing a lay ministry at the Neponsit Home for the Aged. *Dissertation Abstracts International,* July 1979, *40* (1-A), 0312.

Discusses the lay ministers' training in a mini-course on the experience of the elderly. The appendix includes a course design based on a book entitled *Give Comfort to My People.* Tasks of the lay ministers involved visitation and preaching. The intention of the author was to prepare a few who could represent the church and could communicate the Gospel to those confined to a domicile of this sort. (Drew University, 1978.)

327. Ruhbach, G. Vollzüge der Frömmigkeit im Alter. (Religious activity in old age.) *Zeitschrift für Gerontologie,* Jan.-Feb. 1977, *10,* 1014.

Some suggestions on how to arouse and deepen religious awareness and religious practice in a way suited to the elderly.

328. Runions, J. E. Pastoral care of the elderly. *Pastoral Psychology,* March 1972, *23* (222), 39-44.

The minister must be aware of the many facets of the aging process and alert to the strengths and needs of the aged. Pastoral roles suggested by the writer include: (a) guidance for the family of the aging person, (b) adequate group functioning for the elderly, (c) their continued involvement in the life of the church, (d) maintaining a close personal relationship with the elderly person, and (e) extending to the elderly the means of grace.

329. Seitz, M. Das Altwerden des Menschen als Aufgabe der Seelsorge. (Human aging as a task for pastoral care.) *Zeitschrift für Gerontologie,* Jan.-Feb. 1977, *10* (1), 3-9.

The pastor's job is seen as helping the elderly person to understand the aging process and its consequences for living. This article is written in scholarly German (*Gelehrtendeutsch*), which is practically a language unto itself. As for the English summary at the end, it stands in need of its own translation. It was evidently written, in English, by someone whose mother tongue is not English.

330. Semancik, Joseph. Report from the aged: Visitations by the clergy. *Priest*, December 1962, *18*, 1062-65.

Aged persons are said to appreciate visits from the clergy; however, in this study, only 25% of the aged were found to have been visited during the year that preceded the interview.

331. Smith, Bert Kruger. Letter to a new pastor. *Austin Seminary Bulletin* (Faculty ed.), October 1980, 96 (3), 5-14.

This "open letter" offers advice on dealing with the well elderly, with the frail elderly, and with families. The aged are to be encouraged to independence in living, learning, and loving. Stress is laid on the young minister's preparing himself for his own old age.

332. Smith, Theodore Kurtz. Pastoral ministry and the needs of the aging. *Dissertation Abstracts International*, September 1976, *40* (3-A), 1536.

Focuses on pastoral concern for improving the older person's quality of life by helping him/her to recover a sense of integrity and worth. The Christian faith provides untapped resources that can make the aged feel affirmed, respected; their creative contributions can be utilized and despair replaced with hope. The second chapter gives reasons why the church should be interested in the older person; chapter three stresses the need for research into understanding the needs, attitudes, and tendencies of the aged. Case studies from a nursing home in Hawaii deal with the pastoral role. Chapter five describes the characteristics of a program structure and the church's role in activating a plan for making use of the elders' contributions. (School of Theology at Claremont, 1979.)

333. Stene, A. Marlin. Recognizing and serving the spiritual needs of older persons. *Lutheran Social Welfare*, Spring 1971, *2* (1), 15-24.

A Lutheran chaplain describes the program of a pilot training project at Ebenezer Home in Minneapolis, designed to prepare clergymen for pastoral ministry to older persons. However, the first half of the article (originally a paper delivered at the Lutheran Conference on Services to the Aging, Washington, D.C., 1970) is devoted to examining "the dynamics of the aging process, as viewed from the physical, the psychological, and the theological disciplines."

334. Stout, Robert Joe. Our misfit children, young and old. *Christian Century*, March 2, 1977, *94*, 194-96.

How the very young and the very old may help each other. Anecdotes with a point. Partnerships of youth and age are both possible and rewarding.

335. Strom, Kenneth R.   Full life for the elderly. *Christianity Today*, June 21, 1968, *12*, 941-42.

Thoughts on ministering to elderly people. The recently retired need counseling. The elderly in general need a sense of personal integrity. One does not feel completed if one feels left out. It is important to emphasize today, not tomorrow, and to know that someone is listening and cares.

336. Svoboda, Robert. *Altersseelsorge* (Pastoral care of the aged). Donauwörth: Ludwig Auer-Cassianeum, 1961.

One volume in a pastoral series for those directly involved in pastoral ministry. Part 1 lays the foundations; this includes the physical and psychological factors in the aging process, pastoral care, some "theses of Christian gerontology," and sermon outlines. Part 2 bears the subtitle, "Anregungen für Gespräche mit alten Menschen" (hints for conversations with elderly persons).

337. Swaim, William T. The Church's Ministry to Older Adults. *Presbyterian Home News*, Mothers Day Edition 1955, *19*, 7-26.

This is self-described as "a not too fruitful letter to the Presbyterian Church," which went through three successive editions in three years. The point is made that older adults receive less than their share of attention from the Church, though "our number is legion." Observations and suggestions for seminary training, ministry, preparation for old age, sermons, pastoral care, recognition of the older apostolate, social attitudes, deacons, homes for the aged, and courses of study concerning various aspects of dealing with the elderly (list on age 20).

338. Synagogue Council of America.   *The synagogue and the aging.* New York: Synagogue Council of America, 1976.

The fundamental goal of this project was to develop awareness and skills leading to the expansion of synagogue-based services to the aged as a real alternative to institutional care. Barriers for congregational development of programs are identified and recommendations are presented for areas of continued religious sector involvement.

339. Taylor, Robert N., Jr.   Pastoral observations of hospitalized senile patients. *Journal of Pastoral Care*, Summer 1955, 9 (2), 94-98.

An account of a seminarian's efforts and observations as a chaplain on a ward for senile male patients in a state hospital—about 40 men, most of them past seventy. Formal religious attitudes are described, but ministry to such people is seen largely in terms of interpersonal relations.

340. That thy days may be long in the good land: A guide to aging programs for synagogues. Washington, D.C.: National Council on the Aging, 1975.

(*Citation 340 continued*)

This is a "how to" book about programs which a synagogue could sponsor for the aging. Designed for use by rabbis, educators, and volunteers, it also deals with serving the homebound and with outreach to those who are institutionalized. Contents: Why Should Synagogues Be Involved? A Rationale for Synagogue Programming with the Jewish Aging, Planning a Program, Serving the Homebound Elderly, Synagogue-based Group Programs, Reaching Out to the Institutionalized Elderly, Appendices.

341. Tillock, Eugene E., & Scarborough, Bernard. The service role of the Roman Catholic chaplain in long-term patient care. *Concern in the Care of the Aging*, Feb.-May 1978, *4* (4-5), 20-25.

Definition of a chaplain. The general and specific duties of a Roman Catholic chaplain in a long-term care facility. He must serve the needs of patients, and he must promote friendly working relationships with administrators and staff.

342. Underwood, Ralph L. Pastoral care with the elderly. *Austin Seminary Bulletin* (Faculty ed.), Oct. 1980, *96* (3), 15-22.

The stated purpose of this study is to "demonstrate in an informal manner that attention to Scripture and Christian tradition does provide some practical guidance for pastoral care with the elderly." The writer organizes his observations around two headings—"Mutuality: Freedom for Each Other," and "Individuality: Freedom Before Each Other." Pastoral care is "with" the elderly, not "to" them.

343. Unitarian Universalist Women's Federation. The church and creative aging. *The Program Builder*, March 1966.

Suggests that churches and their ministers need to explore profound religious and ethical questions about aging. Segregation of the elderly should not be a goal.

344. United Lutheran Churches of America. *Ye visited me.* New York: United Lutheran Church of America, Board of Social Ministry, 1956.

A guide to "friendly visiting" in a congregation or community. Basic information on what a visitor is to do and why, how visiting helps the homebound aged. This booklet aims at encouraging the practice of lay visitation as a service of the church to aged members.

345. Van Boening, Gary Don. A ministry of the church to the family during the life cycle. *Dissertation Abstracts International*, September 1979, *40* (3-A), 1537.

The author's D. Min. project was to design a model for ministry to the family during the four dominant stages of the life cycle, the last of these stages being the Aged Adult. Dietrich Bonhoeffer's theology of church was used as a conceptual framework. The aged form only a part of this slender study, but they are seen in the context of the whole life cycle, and there is value in that perspective. (School of Theology at Claremont, 1979.)

346. Wiederaenders, Ruth. Social worker and the pastor as a team. *Concordia Theological Monthly*, January 1964, *35*, 26; 32.

Current rethinking of the totality of man emphasizes multidisciplinary approach to meeting total needs. Pastors have been reluctant to work together with social workers for a host of reasons. The caseworker in turn hesitates to work with the pastor. But when both meet in an atmosphere of Christ-like love, their efforts on behalf of their fellowmen should bear fruit. Some practical measures and suggestions. A fourfold program was presented at the Second National Conference on the Church and Social Welfare in 1961.

347. Wygal, Winnifred. To keep a cutting edge. *Social Action*, October 1965, *32*, 28-30.

Churches have always depended on volunteers. Needed now is a redefinition of the work that a volunteer does. Also needed is "a sober and dedicated look" at what elderly people themselves can do. People aged 60 to 85 must be called into this new ministry of the church to the world.

348. Wynn, John Charles. Families and their aged persons. In *Pastoral Ministry to Families*. Philadelphia: Westminster Press, 1957, 153-65.

This chapter in Mr. Wynn's book deals with three special problems in pastoral care, the first of these "families and their aged persons." Practical suggestions are offered both for the minister and for people who have aged persons living with them in their homes: approaches to take, basic human relations, age and satisfaction, money and the aged person, the need for privacy.

IV MISCELLANEOUS TITLES ON RELIGION AND AGING

349. Aging is for all of us: Resources for a church's ministry with older persons. Prepared by a task force of the Homes and Institutions Committee, Pennsylvania Southeast Conference, the United Church of Christ, n.d.

Despite the title, this publication actually imparted information to the aged and their families: books to read, guides for selecting a nursing home, quizzes on aging, etc.

350. Ankenbrandt, Thomas. The church and mature Christians: Reflections on pastoral care for the elderly. *America*, November 13, 1976, *135*, 318-19.

"When will the church do something for the elderly?" Here are suggestions for a parish office or center, full-time coordinator, or for a Christian service corps committed to working with the elderly, the poor, the sick, the oppressed.

351. Argyle, Michael. *Religious behavior.* London: Routledge & Kegan Paul, 1958 (edition consulted). Also, Glencoe, Ill.: The Free Press, 1959.

Contains a chapter on "Religion and Age." The various periods of life are considered briefly in relation to religious experience and beliefs—childhood, adolescence, young adulthood, and "late adulthood, 30 onwards." This "late" adulthood takes up about two pages, the most valuable part of which is a table borrowed from Cavan et al., *Personal Adjustment in Old Age* (Chicago, 1949).

352. Au, Thomas Hardy. The church's role in the problem of aging. *Dissertation Abstracts International*, December 1975, *36* (6-A), 3777.

The problem of aging is seen as exacerbated in our technological society in contrast to biblical times. After developing this point, two chapters are devoted to modern theories of working with the aged and to "pertinent physiological and psychological information from gerontology." The contribution made by theology is described as "questioning the current value system" and as "presenting conceptions of God and religion which can be supportive of a call to . . . . new life styles." The role of the church is taken up in chapter six, where three levels of involvement are suggested. The abstract does not indicate that new information or a definite plan of action is offered. (School of Theology at Claremont, 1975.)

353. Barozzi, Al. Society, church seen ignoring the aged. *National Catholic Reporter*, July 6, 1973, *9*, 2.

Short newspaper article reporting (in somewhat aggressive fashion, as evidenced by the headline chosen) a seminar on aging sponsored by Fordham University in New York. Quotes from Father William Bier, chairman of the psychology department; Father William Hogan, provincial superior of the Holy Cross Society; Sister Rose Mary Strain, director of the Active Retirement Center at Dobbs Ferry, New York; and Samuel Scheiber, a retired businessman.

354. Batzka, David L. *Instruction manual for the older adult church survey project.* Indianapolis: The National Benevolent Association, Division of Social and Health Sciences of the Christian Church (Disciples of Christ), Mimeo. (See also citation 355.)

355. Batzka, David L., & Steele, Paul E. *Coming of age in the Christian church* (Disciples of Christ): *Northeast older adult survey report, August 17, 1973.* Indianapolis: The National Benevolent Association, Division of Social and Health Sciences of the Christian Church (Disciples of Christ), 1973, Mimeo.

The Batzka instruction manual and the Batzka-Steele survey report should be examined together. Both refer to a 1973 study "of the life situations of older persons who are members of several (10) Christian Church congregations in Northeastern Indianapolis." The survey seems to have been done very well and could perhaps serve as a model for similar church inquiries. Out of a possible 1,604 persons over 55 years of age, 368 or 23% were interviewed. "The random sample was taken from three age groups 55-64, 65-74, and 75 and over: 38% from the 55 age group, 29% from the 65 age group, and 33% from the 75 age group." Since the survey was undertaken as a planning tool for the 10 participating churches, the main emphasis of the report is on policy implications and program development.

356. Becker, K. F. Zur Lage zwischen Theologie und empirischer Gerontologie. (Relations between theology and empirical gerontology: Remarks concerning the present situation.) *Zeitschrift für Gerontologie,* Jan.-Feb. 1977, *10* (1), 51-60.

The first part is a brief historical survey reflecting on the advantages and disadvantages of a theory of aging and on the importance of empirical gerontology for practical theology. The second part deals with several special questions upon which theology will have to do a little more pondering. Part 3 is about the elderly in relation to the church's task of adult religious education.

357. Belter, E. W. What does the church expect for its aging? *Professional Nursing Home,* February 1964, 6, 30-34.

Originally a paper which Belter, a Lutheran minister, presented at the Mid-America Nursing Home Convention and Exhibition in Chicago in November of 1963. The church, he says, expects whatever anyone else expects for the aged, *plus.* Adequate physical care is first: adequate facilities and dedicated staff. Of vital concern is the medical staff as well as contractual agreements between nursing homes and local hospitals. Both preventive and restorative therapy are considered important. The church must be concerned with raising standards for all homes; subsidies are needed for this.

358. Bernholz, Adolph. The family and its aged members. *Franciscan Educational Conference*, 1960, *41*, 159-68.

There are sections on support from children in their parents' old age, cautions for the aged, the aged in their own homes, and institutions for the aged.

359. Bibliography on aging and religion and aging. Ontario Department of Social and Family Services, Office on Aging, May 1968, Typescript.

The guiding theme is aging and its implications for theological colleges and training schools. Pages 5 and 6 offer a bibliography on the religious aspect.

360. Blizzard, Samuel L. Expanding the role of organized religion to the aged. In Scudder, Delton L. (Ed.), *Organized religion and the older person.* Gainesville: Univ. of Florida Press, 1958, 91-102.

Discusses organized religion's limited involvement in programming for older persons. In the past, organized religion has largely discharged its responsibility to older persons by establishing homes for the aged. The need for separate institutions for the aged warrants reexamination. Churches and synagogues should consider four features in adjusting their program for the increasing number of old people: give meaning to life, focus on intrapersonal and interpersonal relations, reexamine associational structures with respect to the needs of older persons, actively participate in a clearinghouse for coordinating community resources.

361. Böckle, Franz. Theological-ethical aspects of aging. *Theology Digest*, Autumn 1975, *23*, 235-40. (Condensed from *Arzt und Christ*, 1974, *20* (3-4), 175-85.)

The goal of medicine cannot simply be the lengthening of the life span. Delaying biological decline ought to serve the purpose of a fulfilling life. Old age must not simply be viewed as a deficit model or as a preparation for death; aged people should be urged to accept and fulfill a role in life. From the theological point of view, aging is eternity shining into time. Discusses research priorities, voluntary euthanasia or the right to one's own death, the need to confront death.

362. Boe, Paul A. Role of the Lutheran Hospital in the care of the aged. *Lutheran Social Welfare Quarterly*, March 1964, *4* (1), 31-39.

Emphasizes the importance of the hospital in the care of elderly people. Hospitals should reexamine their functions and resources in order to meet the total needs of the aged in the community. Owing to the special problems of the elderly, special services are required (among which religion is mentioned).

363. Butler, Robert.   Ecumenical efforts to serve the aged. *Hospital Progress*, August 1970, *51*, 94-98.

Indicates that churches must do more. Homes for the aged are islands of concern and care, but are not the total answer. Churches may have to learn how to relinquish excessive identity and learn to work together with other churches, combining resources, planning, pooling skilled manpower. Churches of all denominations can serve as bases for hot meals on wheels, for friendly visitors. [NB: This article, which was originally written as a speech at the 1970 Protestant Health Assembly in Washington, D.C., also includes "components for a national church program of practical ecumenism," and six "objectives for the churches given by Dr. Prescott Thompson."]

364. Church challenged by population profile. *Christian Century*, March 28, 1962, *79* (13), 381.

Population changes, projected over the decade 1962-72, are seen as a challenge to the churches. Doubt is expressed whether the churches recognize and accept this challenge.

365. Clements, William M.   *Care and counseling of the aging.* Philadelphia: Fortress Press, 1979.

A synthesis of up-to-date psychological and theological perspectives about aging, along with practical and theoretical insights. The view presented is that the entire human life cycle offers opportunities for spiritual growth. The writer is a clergyman of the United Methodist Church, as well as a pastoral counselor and assistant professor in the Department of Family Practice at the University of Iowa College of Medicine.

366. Coffy, Archbishop Robert.   La Vie Montante—sens de ce mouvement. (Meaning of "La Vie Montante" movement.) *La Documentation Catholique*, Nov. 16, 1975, *72* (1686), 985-87.

A paper delivered by the Catholic archbishop of Albi at a diocesan assembly of the movement called, "La Vie Montante." Existence is a grace, to be valued for its own sake. The "third age" is a time of rest. [NB: This is a movement for the elderly and the retired: two categories which are closely associated or even identified in much of European thought.]

367. Cottrell, Fred.   Religion. In Cottrell, William F., *Aging and the aged.* Dubuque: Wm. C. Brown Company, 1974, 50-57.

This chapter, in a few short pages, deals with the nature of religion, the religious history of the U.S.A., church attendance, churches meeting the needs of the aged, voluntary organizations in church activity, religion and the fear of death. Given the vast range of topics and the few pages devoted to "religion" as a totality in this 72-page textbook of sociology, the remarks are rather superficial.

368. Creen, Edward, & Simmons, Henry. Toward an understanding of religious needs in aging persons. *Journal of Pastoral Care*, 1977, *31* (4), 273-78.

The subdivisions of this article are as follows: "Aging in Our Society," "The Christian Churches" (survey, in one page, of what the churches are doing for the aged), "Spiritual Tasks of the Aging Person" (integration and life review), "The Role of Faith and the Christian Churches" (hope of eternal life).

369. Cunningham, Sister Agnes. Finding a continuing meaning in life. *Chicago Studies*, Summer 1976, *15*, 139-47.

Written by a theologian, the thrust of this article is the continuing meaning of life combined with a spirituality appropriate to the aging. It is intended to foster discussion within the Catholic church.

370. Davidson, Norman L. Understanding the aged. *Journal of Pastoral Care*, 1958, *12* (1), 17-27.

A description of the aging process, written to serve as background information in ministering to the aged. A popularization, with no really new information—but readable.

371. Davis, Jack A. Programs by church related groups. In Osterbind, Carter C. (Ed.), *Aging: A regional appraisal*. Gainesville: Univ. of Florida Press, 1961, 160-64.

Argues that religion should be concerned about such basic needs as food, shelter, and clothing. It should also provide lifelong opportunities for growth and service and fellowship, in addition to providing the elderly with such services as will keep them close to God and the church in their latter days. Despite the subtitle of the book, there are no specific reports on any church programs in the region.

372. Delloff, Linda M. Combating ageism: agenda for the '80's. *Christian Century*, November 19, 1980, *97*, 1116-18.

The National Interfaith Coalition on Aging convened an ecumenical "inter-sector" (i.e., including non-religious organizations) symposium October 27-30, 1980. Purpose of the symposium was to make White House Conference delegates aware of two points: the importance of the spiritual well-being of the elderly, and that spiritual, ethical, or moral principles should be the basis for *all* issues at the White House Conference on Aging. Recommendations were also made for an "age integrated" society, in which the elderly would not be singled out on the basis of age. The problem of "separation of church and state" that is involved in a religious organization like NICA taking any recommendations to, and being recognized by, the White House Conference comes up at the end of the *Christian Century* report.

373. Delloff, Linda M. Rise up before the hoary head. *Christian Century,* May 2, 1979, 96, 483-85.

A report (in "Editorial Correspondence") on the 8th annual meeting of the National Interfaith Coalition on Aging, held in Nashville from April 9 to 10, 1979. There is a brief history of the NICA, an outgrowth of the 1971 White House Conference on Aging, which included a section on "spiritual well-being." Mention is made of the "GIST" program (Gerontology in Seminary Training), and a discussion of the role of NICA at the 1981 White House Conference. There is a demand "to meet the needs of the total person," and a detailing of four main emphases for the NICA board.

374. Desmond, Thomas C. The new concern for old age. *Christian Century,* December 28, 1960, 77, 1530-32.

This author believes the new concern must go beyond material help for the aged and assist them in finding new social roles. Let them be treated as important members of society and not cast aside.

375. Devaney, Donald. What the old can say to the young: Aging nuns. *Sisters Today,* 1974, 45, 413-19.

Opinions are voiced on the role of the older person in our culture, particularly in a religious community. Older religious should be an example of what religious life can do for human and spiritual growth. Self-actualization is found only in people 60 or older: it is the ultimate state of affairs. It implies the internalization of attitudes, behavior that is consistent. Because of their superior perception, the self-actualized have a clearer notion of right and wrong, a more accurate perception of future events, a deeper humility. There is creativity, dedication, a low degree of self-conflict, enjoyment of life.

376. Duckat, Walter. The attitudes toward the aged in Rabbinic literature. *Jewish Social Services Quarterly,* 1953, 29, 320-24.

The Talmud is drawn upon for sayings about old age and the aged. The aged are to be respected and provided for; however, they are not to abuse their status. At times, the aged did not receive their due. Note is taken in the literature of physical deterioration, also of the connection between diet and longevity, and of grief at the loss of a spouse. Rabbinic literature abounds with references to the fruitful use of time and to the importance of being at the service of others.

377. Dunne, Agnese. Feature X: Apostolate for retired professional lay Catholics. *America,* March 5, 1955, 92, 591-92.

As a Fulbright instructor in Egypt, Dunne was impressed that the mission school for girls in Cairo, under the auspices of the United Presbyterian Church, expected two new faculty members from the U.S.A., both retired school teachers. In the "Feature X" article, she suggests that Catholics do the same. "Many competent oldsters contemplate enforced retirement with a certain rebellion, knowing the contribution they are still very well able to make. . . . Catholic missions have a crying need for doctors, nurses, pharmacists, agricultural specialists, teachers, social workers. . . . We fail to appeal to our men and women in the full-fruited autumn of life."

378. Entman, Sidney. The ministry of organized religion to the Jewish aged—Its philosophy and practice. In Scudder, Delton L. (Ed.), *Organized religion and the older person.* Gainesville: Univ. of Florida Press, 1958, 34-42.

Actually more on the philosophy than on the practice. The Jewish community has always accepted ministry to all human needs as a basic responsibility. The needs of the aged, as a category, are being met by a broad spectrum of services offered by many Jewish communities.

379. Fahey, Charles J. The challenge of aging to the American Church. *Catholic Charities Review,* January 1974, 58, 24-26.

Liberation theology can serve as a frame of reference; namely, the church's responsibility to those whose freedom is diminished. The facilitating process of helping the elderly focus on their needs has just begun. The integration of the elderly into the Christian community leaves much to be desired. The concept of the elderly as ministers of, and witnesses to, the Gospel has hardly been explored.

380. Fahey, Charles. Who is old: A church-state perspective. *Social Thought,* Spring 1976, 2 (2), 2-7.

The "Church perspective" constitutes the second half of this editorial introducing a special issue of *Social Thought.* Msgr. Fahey examines traditional and changing church roles vis-a-vis the elderly in care for the infirm aged and in the administration of sacraments. However, he feels that the most important sector of the elderly population is that of the retiree, whose life and attitude will give either a positive or a negative witness to the Gospel. "We will have failed in our mission if we do not challenge the young-elderly to the fullness of life in the Spirit."

381. Fecher, Con J., & Nix, James T. If only she were a little younger: The impact of aging on religious communities of women. *Linacre Quarterly,* May 1961, 28 (2), 60-63.

The result of decreased vocations and increased longevity is a greater percentage of older Sisters in the community. This study attempts to forecast the effects, administrative, economic and medical. There will be less productivity in terms of school and hospital services and increased expenditures for drugs and infirmary care; the danger of overwork and of obesity, the need for recreation. Sisters may be old chronologically, but they can still be productive if spiritually and psychologically young.

382. Fischer, Edward. Aging as worship. *Worship,* March 1978, 52, 98-108.

(Citation 382 continued)

A tissue of literary allusions, some of which may shed a little light on "worship." The author's entire argument seems to be condensed into these sentences near the end of his article: "Developing an admirable old age is a day-by-day effort of many small victories and some major defeats. Old age, like a vocation, takes on a marvelous shape under the pressure of significant work. It is in the significance that worship lies."

383. Fitch, William C.   Churches and the needs of older persons. *Social Action*, January 1960, *26*, 3-6.

Asks that, although the church may not be able to increase the income of retired workers, it should be aware of their economic status and informed about local resources. Churches have given their greatest support and leadership in the field of housing. Every active church has need of volunteers to implement its programs: the older members could help and want to be asked. Many churches have senior citizen groups. The church can help prepare people for retirement.

384. Foley, James.   Old age for religious: A time of apostolic fruitfulness. *Review for Religious*, January 1975, *34*, 108-12.

"It is the position of these pages that the greatest apostolic fruitfulness in a person's life is in their old age; since that is the time when they are the most poor, the most humble (helpless), the most selfless in prayer, the most united with the Crucified."

385. Foster, Lloyd; Randall, Ollie; & Maves, Paul B.   Later maturity: Panel discussion of a radio play. *Pastoral Psychology*, February 1958, *9*, 29-32.

"The whole social pattern for the future depends on the deepening of understanding between older and younger people." The church has resources to promote this understanding. The radio play which this panel was discussing concerned retirement and the generation gap between a father on the one side and his daughter and son-in-law on the other. The local pastor plays a key role.

386. Frakes, Margaret.   [An eight-part series "on the church and older people."] *Christian Century*, Oct. 19 through Dec. 7, 1955, *72*, 1201-1204; 1233-35; 1268-70; 1297-99; 1329-32; 1366-68; 1397-99; 1426-29.

The first of the eight articles begins on page 1201, the last of them finishes on page 1429. Each article runs three or four pages and has a different title, though all have the same subtitle quoted above.

1. "Multiplied in the Land" (Oct. 19, 1201-04): The increase of aging persons in the United States and their problems. 2. "A Refuge and Strength" (Oct. 26, 1233-35): Spiritual needs of older men and women. 3. "Forsake Me Not" (Nov. 2, 1268-70): What are American denominations doing? 4. "Fellowship in Ministering" (Nov. 9, 1297-99): Interchurch efforts. 5. "Life

More Abundantly" (Nov. 16, 1329-32): Golden Age Clubs as a tool for church efforts; church-offered facilities. 6. "Their Days Renewed" (Nov. 23, 1366-68): Other programs. 7. "A Desired Haven" (Nov. 30, 1397-99): Church-established homes for the aged. 8. "If Ye Have Not Love" . . . (Dec. 7, 1426-29): more or less a continuation of part 7, but adds suggestions on how to improve facilities in homes for the aged.

387. Frommelt, H. A new apostolate for senior citizens. *Our Sunday Visitor*, November 5, 1972, *61*, 1.

All levels of experience of retired persons, from laboring to administration, could be used in the church. Calls for an organization that could offer seminars to prepare for retirement and could publish a catalogue of second careers in parish, home, and foreign missions.

388. Gorry, Edward Joseph. *Attitudes toward work and retirement among male religious clergy.* Washington, D.C.: Cara, 1979.

A master's thesis in gerontology at the University of Southern California. One of the institutional changes brought about by Vatican II was the recommendation that retirement be considered for religious personnel. This study focuses on one religious order of ordained clergymen and seeks to examine the attitudes of members towards work and towards retirement. These clergymen "attributed intrinsic value to the meaning of their priestly work," but such work "does not occupy a position of central life interest" for them. If there is an opportunity for continued priestly work, they will choose to work even after reaching retirement age.

389. Gratton, Carolyn. Summaries of books relevant to the topic of spirituality and aging. Selected bibliography on the topic of spirituality and aging. *Studies in Formative Spirituality*, November 1980, *1*, 481-95.

From page 481 to page 488, the following books are given an extended review a little more than one page long (each): Blythe, Ronald, *The View in Winter: Reflections on Old Age*, New York, 1979. Haughton, Rosemary, *The Catholic Thing*, Springfield, Ill., 1977. Levinson, Daniel J. *The Seasons of a Man's Life*, New York, 1978. Tournier, Paul, *Learning To Grow Old*, London, 1972. Whitehead, Evelyn E. and Whitehead, James D., *Christian Life Patterns: The Psychological Challenges and Religious Invitations to Adult Life*, New York, 1979. Van Kaam, Adrian, *The Transcendent Self: Formative Spirituality of the Middle, Early, and Later Years of Life*, Denville, New Jersey, 1979.

Pages 489-495 simply list books without notes under the following headings: Maturational Dimensions of the Aging Process (24 books); Formative Literature Related to Aging from the Catholic Tradition (27); Social and Cultural Directives for Aging (27); Religion and Death in Relation to Aging (20); Old Age as a Theme in World Literature (26); Directives on Aging from a Number of Disciplines (31); Incarnational Aspects of Aging from a Scientific Viewpoint (24).

390. Graying of the Church: A problem and an opportunity. A Report of the U.S.C.C. Dialogue on Aging. *Hospital Progress*, May 1980, *61*, 24.

The initials U.S.C.C. stand for United States Catholic Conference. The U.S. Catholic Bishops' Committee on Social Development and World Peace convened a "dialogue on meeting the needs of the elderly," so that those active in ministering to the elderly could make recommendations to the committee. The church's efforts, it was felt, must focus on two ministries: *to* the elderly and *of* the elderly. Msgr. Charles Fahey outlined five pastoral principles given in this article; they are too complex to be reproduced in this note.

391. Guinan, Sister St. Michael. Aging and religious life. *Gerontologist*, 1972 (#1, pt.1), 21.

The writer calls for a study of motivation and aging in the religious life, from the standpoint of developmental psychology. Aging religious (nuns) are seen as part of the retirement problem.

392. Guttmann, David. Leisure-time activity interests of Jewish aged. *Gerontologist*, 1973, *13* (4), 219-23.

Two different groups of Jewish aged, the native and the foreign-born, have different interests in the leisure activities which are offered by community centers. It is important to have a cultural understanding of ethnic groups before planning activities for the elderly.

393. Heenan, Edward F. Aging in religious life. *Review for Religious*, November 1968, *27*, 1120-27.

Social factors relating to aging in the general population, aging and the religious institution, two theories of aging (disengagement and Rose's interaction theory), community vs. bureaucracy. What do the elderly want? To live as long as possible, to preserve waning physical energies, to safeguard prerogatives acquired in midlife, to remain active in the affairs of life, to withdraw from life honorably and comfortably. The closer the community approaches the ideal of integrating and providing for the needs of each member, the more successful the aging process. On the other hand, the more bureaucratized the community, the greater the estrangement during the aging process. [NB: In this context, a "religious" is a person leading a consecrated life under vows recognized by the Catholic Church; the "community" is the order or local group to which they belong.]

394. Herold, Sister Duchesne. *New life: Preparation of religious for retirement.* St. Louis: Catholic Hospital Association, 1973.

[NB: See the preceding note for the concept of "a religious."] The members of (Catholic) religious orders do not completely withdraw from the kind of work they knew, but simply use their God-given talents in another way. Chapter 2 in particular is devoted to developing a retirement program for such religious persons, and Chapter 4 to preparing them for retirement. Chapter 5 sketches a spirituality of aging.

395. Heschel, Abraham. *To grow in wisdom.* New York: Synagogue Council of America, 1961.

Professor Heschel's address delivered at the 1961 White House Conference on Aging. This pamphlet carries the following subheadings: The Test of a People, Individual Benevolence and Community Responsibility, The Trivialization of Existence, The Sense of Being Useless to Society, The Sense of Inner Emptiness and Boredom, Education for Retirement, Loneliness and Fear of Time, The Moment Is the Marvel, The Meaning of the Family, The Sense of Significant Being.

396. Hickey, Tom. Catholic religious orders and the aging process: Research, training, and service program. *Gerontologist,* 1972, *12* (#1, pt. 1), 16-17.

About Catholic orders of religious women (nuns) and the aging process. Difficulties are caused by the Protestant work ethic, by the generation gap, by the recent turmoil which has caused many Sisters to question their own personal commitment. This short article on an immense question ends with hopes for more research, for adult education, for service programs.

397. Hickey, Thomas, & Kalish, Richard A. The new old nuns: The changing life patterns of Catholic Sisters. *Gerontologist,* 1969, *9* (#3, pt. 1), 170-78.

This paper takes soundings, at no great depth, of the changes occurring among Catholic religious orders of Sisters and the implications thereof for elderly Sisters. A new type of elderly nun is emerging, according to the writers, more in keeping with modern times and modern ideas about work and retirement. This has required a rethinking of the mores and values in vogue when those nuns were socialized. The writers note that they interviewed 70 Sisters who belonged to 25 different orders—which sounds impressive until one checks out the official Catholic Directory for 1969. In that year, there were more than 167,000 Catholic nuns divided into 494 different orders and spread across 50 states. The nuns Hickey and Kalish interviewed were all on the West Coast.

398. Hickey, Tom, & Kalish, Richard A. American Catholic Sisters and the aging process. *Proceedings, 77th Annual Convention of the American Psychological Association,* 1969, 739-40.

The fifty subjects for this study, ranging in age from 45 to 85 years, were chosen on a nonrandom basis. The first phase of the study consisted of a series of semistructured depth interviews with 20 administrators and superiors from selected orders of Sisters on the West Coast. The second phase was a mail survey of opinions and viewpoints of 30 pre-selected Sisters from different parts of the U.S.A. "There was strong evidence of an emerging awareness among Catholic Sisters in the United States of their own problems in the aging process. . . . There is also a new emphasis on second careers, adult education programs, and the development of proper roles for elderly members." (See also citation 397.)

399. Hiltner, Seward. A theology of aging. In Scudder, Delton L. (Ed.), *Organized religion and the older person.* Gainesville: Univ. of Florida Press, 1958, 1-11.

"Theology" means the attempt to understand, state, and clarify the meaning of faith in its basic aspects. The older years involve loss in some kinds of powers. How does a theology of aging deal with the fact of loss? What do faith and theology have to say about grief and bereavement? Then, our theology of aging deals with the free cultivation of fulfillment in its depth dimension. Another point is the meaning of vocation and of responsibility in older years.

400. Hiltner, Seward. Facts and needs: Present and future. *Pastoral Psychology,* Winter 1975, *24* (229), 97-101.

After quoting some current facts and figures, Hiltner points out seven trends suggesting the need for theological reflection. These are: the steady increase in the over-65 population; an increase in vitality among older people, which makes them capable of productive work; the existence of a "learning period" during which aging can be "taught" in years earlier than 65; the fact that older women will greatly outnumber older men; the need to reconsider both work and leisure; the discrimination against all underprivileged groups that must be eliminated; the change in our culture's present ambivalent attitudes towards both aging and older people.

401. Hogan, William F. The challenge of aging for contemporary religion. In Bier, William C. (Ed.), *Aging: Its challenge to the individual and to society.* New York: Fordham Univ. Press, 1974, 26-34.

To devote attention solely to programs for the elderly would be to remain on the surface. Religion must address itself more deeply to the process of life and the development of a life vision. The functional values of American society are examined for their influence on those approaching old age. Old age is seen as a potential for growth; stress is laid on the value of leisure and on a reverence for life itself. Finally the church's ministry to the aged is considered in terms of programs to meet the needs of the elderly and to utilize their wisdom with a stronger thrust needed toward pastoral counseling for the dying.

402. Holbrook, T.   Senior citizens in the Mystical Body. *Hospital Progress,* April 1963, *44,* 78-79.

The average person, the business world, the government, and fund-raising organizations have all tended to ignore old age. Our attitudes must change. The senior members of our community should be treated with honor. Pope Pius XII and Pope John XXIII are quoted.

403. Howie, Carl G.   Theology for aging. In Thorson, James A., & Cook, Thomas C., Jr. (Eds.), *Spiritual well-being of the elderly.* Springfield, Ill.: Charles C. Thomas, 1980, 64-70.

The purpose here is to discover how the affirmation of theology should inform the aging experience: God, Christ, redemption, life seen as steward-ship, responsibility towards others. There is a peculiar stewardship for the aged—they show that life has a value in and of itself, and they remind the rest of society what the lasting realities are. Finally, death is not destruction but fulfillment.

404. Hunter, Woodrow W.   Leadership training for pre-retirement pro-grams in religious communities. *Gerontologist,* 1972, *12* (#1, pt. 1), 17-19.

Retirement needs in religious communities were studied by five religious Sisters from college faculties in the state of Michigan. The purpose was to help formulate retirement education programs in religious orders. Sugges-tions were made for a retirement committee and for retirement training centers. Despite the title, this article deals with the workshops having been held more than about any actual training of the leadership. It demonstrates the need for pre-retirement programs rather than gives details about existing ones or about how to structure them.

405. Indiana Commission on the Aging and the Aged.   *Religion in the life of the aging and the aged.* State of Indiana, 1965. Proceedings of the Seventh Annual Conference on Aging.

Papers given at the conference and printed in the Proceedings include: "The Creative Challenge of Aging," by Rabbi Rudolph M. Rosenthal; "Creative Involvement—Riverside Church and Older Adults," by Alice M. Pattie; "Role of the Church and Synagogue in Community Programs for the Aging," by Esther C. Stamats; "The Real Needs of Older People," by Herchel Hollopeter; "Preparing for the Later Years," by Virginia Stafford. The latter includes a subsection on, "How the church or synagogue can help persons prepare for later maturity." The booklet ends with a "Summary" by Dr. Grover Hartman, Executive Secretary of the Indiana Council of Churches.

406. Jean, Sister Gabrielle L.   Religious congregations and service to the elderly. *Review for Religious,* 1978, *37,* 612-18.

This article focuses on the needs of the aging population in America with a view to exploring how religious congregations (orders, especially of nuns) can respond to those needs: day care centers, sheltered housing, escort services, visitation.

407. Johnson, Gerald K. Spiritual aspects of aging. *Lutheran Social Welfare Quarterly*, 1964, *4* (3), 28-36.

Discusses the older person's remaining life task as the struggle of integrity with despair and disgust. Disruptive forces in the aging process are matched with the integrating power of the grace of God. The church is obligated to the whole man. A definition of the "spiritual" effects of disruptive cultural changes, the doings of the inner man.

408. Kanouse-Roberts, Aliça L. A study of the interaction between a group of Jewish senior citizens and a group of Black adolescent girls classified as delinquent. *Dissertation Abstracts International*, January 1978, *38* (7-A), 2892.

A case study designed to explore helpful methods for overcoming the negative effects of being known as deviants or fearful old people. Three months of face-to-face interaction between 17 Black adolescents and a number of senior citizens produced significant positive changes for the young girls, and both groups became more tolerant.

409. Katz, Robert L. Jewish values and sociopsychological perspectives on aging. In Hiltner, Seward (Ed.), *Toward a theology of aging.* New York: Human Sciences Press, 1975, 135-50.

The Jewish approach to aging is constructive. Old age can be the "sabbath" of human life. If a man no longer works, guilt is inappropriate. Fundamental social change is needed; old age should be the high point of the human career.

410. Kohlberg, Lawrence. Stages and aging in moral development: Some speculations. *Gerontologist*, 1973, *13* (4), 497-502.

The writer extrapolates from findings on adult moral-stage development, "to raise the possibility of stage development in old age." Six moral stages are outlined, leading up to early adulthood. Stage number 7 is postulated as something that follows a "post-conventional faith," and it answers a religious question. Kohlberg raises the possibility that "the field of aging could find some of its most unique and deepest problems emerging from philosophical concepts rather than from the more usual concepts of biology and social sciences."

411. La Farge, John. On turning seventy: A time for prayer, charity, and courage. *America*, November 18, 1961, *106*, 242-45.

Written at a time when the author, a well-known Jesuit priest and journalist, was 82 years of age. "It is important that we approach this period fortified with a definite purpose and program. . . . That prayer become more and more a part of the texture of our lives. . . . Old age is a time for charity. . . . The third factor is courage. The later years are a time of diminution; they preface the total diminution which ends life itself. Courage consists in accepting this diminution as it comes."

412. The later years: A new phase in the life cycle. *Social Thought*, Spring 1976, 2 (2), 2-80.

This issue of *Social Thought* examines the aging phenomenon from several perspectives and critically analyzes some current social, economic, and cultural factors which contribute to their being a problem. Contents of the issue: "Who Is Old: A Church-State Perspective" by Charles Fahey, "Respect for Age in Christianity: The Base of Our Concern in Scripture and Tradition" by Kenneth R. Knapp; "The Later Years: A Psychological Perspective" by Steven R. Steury, MD; "The Later Years: An Applied Sociological Approach" by William A. Maesen; "More Years or More Life" by Lorraine Hashian; "Higher Education and the Older Adult" by Vivian Wood and Beth Trachtenberg; "Legal-Social Services: Meeting Needs and Protecting Rights" by Johanna E. McCarthy.

413. Living abundantly: The later years—new opportunities for church ministry. New York: Executive Council of the Protestant Episcopal Church, 1967.

This pamphlet was prepared "in the hope that it will bring into sharper focus our understanding of the problems of older persons today and of how the church can contribute constructively towards their solution." Needs, objectives, church resources supporting independent living (homemakers, friendly visiting, meals-on-wheels, group programs). Church resources for long-term care.

414. Londoner, Carroll A. Survival needs of the older church member: Implications for educational programming. *Pastoral Psychology*, May 1971, 22, 14-20.

Educational programs for older adults must be developed to help them acquire new competencies to meet the new demands that emerge. In the section on "instrumental education for survival in the later years," the writer lists five categories of needs: financial, health, continued work opportunities, familial relationships, and personal needs. Pastors and church education planners should keep these needs of the elderly in view.

415. Lott, J. Die Religionspädagogik und das Alter. (Religious education and old age.) *Zeitschrift für Gerontologie*, Jan.-Feb. 1977, 10 (1), 26-36.

A philosophy of religious education based on Paulo Freire's idea that an oppressed people learn only in a conflict situation. The elderly, too, must learn to understand their condition in the subculture of the aged and to work out their conflicts with the social environment.

416. Lovely, Sister Marie Laurette. The experience of a retired nun. In Bier, William C. (Ed.), *Aging: Its challenge to the individual and to society.* New York: Fordham Univ. Press, 1974, 174-75.

One modest page on the life of a retired teaching nun.

417. MacGuigan, J. E. The aging religious priest. *Gerontologist,* 1972, *12* (#1, pt. 1), 19-20.

Though this paper claims to cover some 3,000 priests belonging to various Catholic religious orders, there are no references to any published sources. The writer thinks he discovers evidence of the "Protestant work ethic" and of "subtle pride" and of "false masculinity" in the idea of "dying in the harness." He wants more emphasis placed on retirement-to rather than on retirement-from; second and third careers should be explored. Each order should have a director of retirement and retirement funds. A congress of all priests over 65 should be held in each order.

418. McCarty, Shaun. Growing old gracefully. *Sisters Today,* November 1974, *46*, 132-41.

A middle-aged priest writes about spirituality for the elderly. Live for today, rather than in the past or the future. Aging can be a special time for prayer. Growing old gives us a better chance to say "I give up" to the Lord. Age should be a time of healing. There is service and witness to be rendered by the aging, who are the bearers of tradition.

419. McGreevy, Sister Mary Virginia. The aged Catholics in two cities: A comparative analysis of social factors and the theory of disengagement. *Dissertation Abstracts International,* October 1966, *27* (4-A), 1122.

A comparison of Catholics 65 years of age and older in Portland, Oregon, and Fort Wayne, Indiana. The section on disengagement deals only with the Portland sample. The religious life of the subjects of this investigation does not loom large at least in the abstract.

420. Masse, Benjamin. The experience of a retired priest. In Bier, William C. (Ed.), *Aging: Its challenge to the individual and to society.* New York: Fordham Univ. Press, 1974, 168-72.

A realistic, balanced view of mandatory retirement as it affected this author, a renowned Jesuit journalist and expert in social questions, when he was retired from active duty by his superiors.

421. Mathiasen, Grace. *The role of religion in the lives of older people.* New York: Governor's Conference on Problems of Aging, 1955, Mimeo.

A background paper prepared for the New York State Governor's Conference on the Problems of Aging. Contents include: The Role of the Church, Rites of the Church and the Practice of Religion, Chaplaincy Service, Pastoral Counseling, Social Service Under Religious Auspices, Homes for the Aged, Foster Homes Program, Friendly Visiting Program, Including Older People in the Church Program of Sociability and Social Service, Golden Age Clubs and Social Centers, Pulpit, Group Programs, Using Community Resources.

422. Maves, Paul B. Research on religion in relation to aging. In Jeffers, F. C. (Ed.), *Duke University Council on Gerontology Proceedings of Seminars, 1961-1965.* Durham: Duke University, 1965, 69-79.

Expresses that there are paradoxes, or contradictions, discernible in reported research on religion and aging; some major deficiencies of this research. Clarifying religion as a subject for research (definition), sketching a model of human development, suggesting some hypotheses which might be explored concerning the religious experience of elderly people.

423. Menkin, Eva L. Dignity in Aging: Notes on geriatric ethics—comment. *Journal of Humanistic Psychology,* 1978, *18* (2), 55-56.

Comment on Christiansen's idea of dignity as applied to the aged: It fits all who are victims of prejudice—and in our culture, the old are victims of prejudice. They can do nothing about it except face it with dignity and defiance. It is the rest of us who need to examine our prejudices and work through our fears of aging.

424. Moberg, David O. Growing old in Christ: A survey of books on aging. *Christianity Today,* November 21, 1980, *24,* 40-41, and December 12, 1980, *24,* 46 (sequential page numbering 1430-1431 and 1504).

Books on aging are reviewed by David O. Moberg in two issues of this magazine. Part I, in the November 21 number, groups books under the headings, General Surveys, Retirement Planning Resources, and Problems of Middlescence. Part II, in the December 12 number, surveys books about Resources for Lay and Professional Leaders and books about Spiritual Health. There is also a section on textbooks.

425. Moberg, David O. *Inasmuch. Christian responsibility in the twentieth century.* Grand Rapids: Wm. B. Eerdmans Publishing Co., 1965.

Moberg writes about the biblical basis for social concern, the needs of society, and the means for implementing and evaluating programs designed to meet these needs.

426. Moberg, David O. Religion in the later years. In Hoffman, Adeline M. (Ed.), *The daily needs and interests of older people.* Springfield, Ill.: Charles C. Thomas, 1970, 175-91.

After introductory remarks, the author discusses the "functions and dysfunctions of religion," practices, feelings, beliefs, knowledge, results, and a sixth "spiritual component." In a third section is a listing of ways in which the church can serve older people, and vice versa.

427. Moberg, David O.   Reflections on the church and the needs of the aging. *Pastoral Psychology*, June 1971, *22*, 54-57.

Moberg believes that the church has more opportunity to influence the well-being of the aged than any other institution through its congregations, clergy, theological schools, and church-related agencies. The aged want spiritual guidance; even those who do not want it have certain needs which they do not recognize. The importance of professional preparation of clergy; volunteer service by seminarians.

428. Moberg, David O.   Spiritual well-being: Background. In *Backgrounds and issues series, Vol. 13, White House Conference on Aging 1971.* Washington, D.C.: U.S. Govt. Printing Office, 1971.

Nature and scope of the "spiritual." A list of six spiritual needs of the aging. Long-range goals: from the Bible, from conferences on aging, from religious bodies. Five major categories of goals for spiritual well-being. Knowledge available about religious practices, beliefs, knowledge, and experiences. The present situation, including deficiencies of present programs.

429. Moberg, David O.   What the graying of America means to the local church. *Christianity Today*, November 20, 1981, *25*, 30-33.

Maintains that the church is the best institutional friend of the elderly. Integrating the elderly into the overall life of the congregation is all right, but aging members have special needs. There are also many possible ministries for the aging to engage in, so that they too can use their spiritual gifts for the benefit of the entire body. To begin ministry in the midst of a graying population, a number of steps are advised: discovering the facts, identifying resources, evaluating their extent, planning for action. Amid all activities, the church should make spiritual well-being central.

430. Morgan, John H. *Aging in the religious life: A comprehensive bibliography, 1960-75.* Wichita, Kans.: Institute on Ministry and the Elderly, Kansas Newman College, 1977.

Bibliographical entries on: aging and religious life, aging and society, aging and health care, aging and retirement, death and dying, national organizations in the field of aging. This listing is more selective than comprehensive.

431. National Council on the Aging. *Report on the policy recommendations of the White House Conference on Aging 1971.* Washington, D.C.: NCOA, 1972.

NCOA was given the responsibility of surveying the implementation of the 1971 WHCOA policy recommendations. As a first step, the NCOA wrote a monograph reorganizing and summarizing the policy recommendations of the conference. The material on "spiritual well-being" is presented on six pages; but it is not easy to locate because the pages of this volume (size: 8½″ x 11″ and 1″ thick) are not numbered consecutively. Nine recommendations are made about "meeting the spiritual needs of the aged"; 15 about "services and spiritual concerns"; and 1 for a "Conference follow-up."

432. Naus, Peter. The elderly as prophets. *Hospital Progress*, May 1978, 59, 66-68.

A prophet calls people from the preoccupations of daily existence to look at the deeper meaning of life. The elderly are in a position to remind others of the temporal nature of existence and to help them find its deeper meaning. The writer devotes much space to his consideration that allowing the elderly to be our teachers and ministers requires a willingness to face up to our own aging and mortality, as well as a willingness to confront stereotypes of our cultural climate, which views aging as progressive deterioration.

433. Nix, James T., & Fecher, Con J. Care of the aging. In *Stamina for the apostolate.* Washington, D.C.: Cara, 1970, 83-89.

Senior religious are limited in work and often require nursing care and hospitalization. They merit appreciation; they want love. A modern religious community should develop a philosophy of aging, envisioning the functioning potential of the elderly. This article attempts some future projections and urges planning on individuals and on religious communities.

434. Nouwen, Henri J. M., & Gaffney, Walter J. *Aging: The fulfillment of life.* Garden City: Doubleday and Co., 1974. Doubleday Image Book ed., 1976.

A spiritual essay, with photographs, on the meaning of aging. It is a popularly written book, intended not so much for scholars as for the general public; its appeal is to the affective side of human nature, rather than to the intellectual. Throughout, the tone is definitely and unabashedly religious. "Moving and inspirational thoughts on what aging means to all of us," as the back cover phrases it.

435. O'Connell, Patrick. The aged apostolate. *Hospital Progress*, October 1966, 47, 69; 82-83.

Emphasizes the dignity and worth of each human being, regardless of his or her condition. Working with the elderly calls for a special kind of vocation, a complete dedication of one's self. The importance of preparing for this vocation as it will be exercised in extended care facilities. Giving confidence to the elderly who have begun to doubt their own worth. All possible spiritual means should be made available to the residents.

436. Papa, Mary Baker. The church in action: Aging. *National Catholic Reporter*, April 15, 1977, *13* (25), 1; 4-5; 20; continued April 22, 1977, *13* (26), 5; 8; 20.

A two-part analysis of the situation: the problem of aging and the church's response, nationwide. The church's aid to the elderly is changing. Political and moral roles are questioned and the aging challenge the church. Although this two-part article appeared in successive issues of a weekly newspaper, it is extensive.

437. Poehlmann, H. G.   Die Altenarbeit der Kirchen unter besonderer Berücksichtigung der Altenbildung. (The churches' work with the elderly, with special consideration of education for the elderly.) *Zeitschrift für Gerontologie*, Jan.-Feb., 1977, *10* (1), 15-25.

This essay develops a plan for the continuing education of elderly Protestants in Germany. After critically examining the findings of empirical gerontology and proposing a "metatheory" of aging from a Christian standpoint, the author draws some possible conclusions for the church's process of Christian education. He also feels that the church should be an advocate for the elderly, speaking out against prejudices and arousing the aged's feeling of self-worth.

438. Proceedings of the Institute on Planning for Pre-Retirement and Retirement of Priests, New Orleans, January 19-21, 1969.   Washington, D.C.: National Conference of Catholic Charities.

This is a collection of papers delivered at the above-mentioned institute. The purpose of the gathering was twofold: "To make those responsible for planning for older priests aware of the comprehensive aspects . . . in a program to meet their total needs and to stimulate interest so that social or regional groups would carry on similar institutes." Included in the New Orleans meeting were some sessions on financing and some on various patterns of living arrangements.

439. Pruyser, Paul W.   Aging: Downward, upward, or forward. In Hiltner, Seward (Ed.), *Toward a theology of aging*. New York: Human Sciences Press, 1975, 102-18. Also in *Pastoral Psychology*, Winter 1975, *24*, 102-18.

Aging is seen as loss, decline, a downhill course. But there are also gains; many persons enjoy getting older. After a description of aging's gains and losses, the writer concludes that the course of life is neither downward nor upward, but a forward movement full of new discoveries.

440. Regan, Thomas F.   Working with our senior citizens. *Catholic Charities Review*, February 1962, *46*, 25-28.

Changes in population age, in the family, and in our industrial culture have created problems for the aged. Every member of the St. Vincent de Paul Society should develop a vital interest in the welfare of senior citizens who live on limited income or who have exhausted their resources. This concern is a way of showing them gratitude for their past efforts and showing them also that they are not forgotten.

441. Reisch, Harold W. The church and the aged: An appraisal. *Lutheran Social Welfare Quarterly*, June 1962, 2 (2), 9-15.

An appraisal of the several factors which should be considered as the church seeks to carry forward its responsibility to the aged in contemporary society. For instance: Institutional care is no longer the primary method; the economic level of aging has improved; long-term or chronic illness is now a major problem; commercial nursing homes have been established; unused time has increased; and patterns of noninstitutional services are emerging.

442. Religious and retirement: Adding new life to years. Washington, D.C.: Proceedings of General Sessions, Georgetown University, July 17-21, 1972, Mimeo.

The proceedings were cosponsored by the National Conference of Catholic Charities and the School for Summer and Continuing Education of Georgetown University. The texts of five papers delivered at the above-mentioned gatherings: "Spiritual Development," by Charles J. Fahey; "Pre-retirement and Retirement Planning," by Sister Marie Gaffney; "The Social-Psychological Aspect of Aging," by Paul Kerschner; "New Life Through Leisure," by Sister Rose Mary Strain; "The Social Responsibility of Older Persons," by Paul Kerschner.

443. Robb, Thomas Bradley. *The bonus years: Foundations for ministry with older persons.* Valley Forge, Pa.: Judson Press, 1968.

An attempt to relate the resources of the local church to the needs of older persons. Scope of the problem, characteristics of aging, the role of the church, getting started. The eleven-page annotated bibliography will be helpful, but it covers more works on aging in general than it does works on the specifically religious or church aspects of the problem.

444. Rossmoor-Cortese Institute for the Study of Retirement and Aging. *Religion and aging: The behavioral and social sciences look at religion and aging.* Los Angeles: Univ. of Southern California, 1967.

Part 1: "An Introduction to the Study of Retirement and Aging," by John E. Cantellon. Part 2: "A Summary of Research Issues in the Discussion of Religion and Aging," by Maurice B. Hamovitch. Part 3: "Religion and Human Needs," by Raymond G. Kuhlen; "Some Findings and Insights from My Research on Religion and Aging," by David O. Moberg; "Religion and Creative Aging," by Ada B. Stough; "Approaches to the Study of Religion and Aging," by Wendell M. Swenson.

445. Sandven, Joe Morris. The local church in service to the senior adult. *Dissertation Abstracts International*, September 1977, 38 (3-A), 1464.

A Doctor of Ministry dissertation. Sociological and theological reflections on the aging problem. The church is called to sensitize the community to the needs of the elderly and to assist them in maintaining a maximum level of participation in life. The church is also encouraged to offer a course entitled, "Planning Your Own Retirement Center," and courses for personal development involving the aging together with younger members of the congregation in a group growth experience. Such a course is outlined in this dissertation.

446. Sauer, Stephen F. (Ed.). *The aging: A religious responsibility.* Austin, Texas: Governor's Committee on Aging, 1975.

This publication is difficult to classify and still more difficult to summarize. Containing reports, charts, outlines, messages, advertisements and memoranda, it seems to be a collection of papers connected in one way or another with an "aging" project sponsored by the Texas Conference of Churches in 1975. The subtitle is, "Learning from a Process Analysis." There are chapters on: Project Design and Authorization, Participant Selection, Regional Team Events, Central Event Preparation, The Central Event, Evaluation Activities, Regional Efforts. There are nineteen appendices, one of which is a speech on "The Aging: A Religious Responsibility," by Dr. Arthur S. Flemming, U.S. Commissioner for Aging.

447. Schumacher, Henry C. The meaning of religion to older people—the psychiatric viewpoint. In Scudder, Delton L. (Ed.), *Organized religion and the older person.* Gainesville: Univ. of Florida Press, 1958, 71-77.

Two pages of discussion about what "religion" means, followed by a discussion of biological and psychological growth patterns. Next, the role of the family; then, old age and our society; finally, some general remarks on "dealing with the whole man." Despite the title of Schumacher's paper, the psychiatric aspects of old age are mentioned only briefly and tangentially.

448. Scudder, Delton L. (Ed.). *Organized religion and the older person.* A report on the Eighth Annual Southern Conference on Gerontology, held at the University of Florida, April 10-11, 1958. Gainesville: Univ. of Florida Press, 1958.

Contents: "A Theology of Aging," by Seward Hiltner; "The Role of Religion and Religious Institutions in Creating the Milieu of Older People," by Milton L. Barron; "The Ministry of Organized Religion to the Jewish Aged—its philosophy and practice," by Sidney Entmen; "The ministry of organized religion to the aged," by Gordon Poteat; "The Meaning of Religion to Older People—The Social Aspect," by Ruth Albrecht; "The Meaning of Religion to Older People—The Psychiatric Viewpoint," by Henry C. Schumacher; "The Meaning of Religion to Older People—The Medical Perspective," by Nila Kirkpatrick Covalt; "Expanding the Role of Organized Religion to the Aged," by Samuel L. Blizzard; "Conference Summary," by Delton Scudder; "Bibliography," by Margaret Knox.

449. Shapero, Sanford M. Vintage years: General view and Jewish challenge. *Journal of Religion and Health*, April 1975, *14* (2), 130-41.

Needs, the puzzle of "geron," early retirement, the professional scene, the cultural vacuum, the Jewish retired person. Although this article is written from the Jewish standpoint, by a retired rabbi, most of the remarks have a more general application.

450. Siefert, Brother E. Growing old in the religious life. *Cross and Crown*, December 1973, *25*, 392-96.

Senior members of [Catholic] religious orders find so many of the traditions having been swept aside. Yet, the senior religious member has faith that he can make it to the end, even in a decimated congregation. Personal prayer is the essence of moral survival. The mellowing religious is advised not to sell his experience short: Let him speak his mind, for he has something valuable to contribute.

451. Smith, R. Spiritual growth in the later years: John XXIII on death and aging. *Review for Religious*, November 1978, *37*, 822-33.

The teaching of Pope John XXIII on the spirituality of the later years, as illustrated from his book, *Journal of a Soul*. There is a summary on page 832, in seven points.

452. Springfield, T. Are churches meeting the needs of older people? In Dixon, James C. (Ed.), *Continuing education in the later years*. Gainesville: Univ. of Florida Press, 1963, 41-50.

"The church, like the rest of our institutions, places a high premium on youth. . . . Compensation for our guilt by making them comfortable. . . . Church-built and sponsored homes for the aged now number about 700. . . . Churches, like other organizations, got busy keeping oldsters busy . . . 'Take care of their physical needs, and keep their minds away from the real problem.' There is convincing evidence that this is not the answer. . . . The church can and should help prepare people of all ages to live with the problem . . . and to prepare for death."

453. Stafford, Virginia. *Older adults in the church.* New York: Methodist Publishing House, 1953.

Contents: America is growing up; a look at the older person; bringing older adults into the church fellowship; older adults, learners; fun and fellowship; older adults serving others; older adults at worship; effective program planning and administration.

454. Stagg, Frank. Biblical perspectives on aging. Athens, Ga.: National Interfaith Coalition on Aging, 1978.

Frank Stagg, a professor of New Testament at a Baptist theological seminary, gave this address at the Southern Baptist Conference on Aging held in Nashville in 1974. Biblical perspectives on length of life, wisdom of age, worth of persons, youth and the aged. Final reflections on youth, maturity, senility, and care of the aged.

455. Stamats, Esther C. Fulfillment years. *Pastoral Psychology*, May 1968, *19*, 33-36.

Written by a 75-year-old, this article is on "the autumn of life" and how religion can help. It is the concern of religion that each individual live as an integrated person, realizing his full potential, because every person deserves this opportunity as a child of God. The religious fellowship is a family in which there are no age limits, no retirements. The older one becomes, the fewer friends and relatives remain, leaving emptiness and loneliness. Here the church is the only substitute for family and friends. Many churches are planning creative ways of involving older persons in all church activities.

456. Suedkamp, Wilbur E., & Jacobs, William J. Old age: Tragedy or gift of God? *Ave Maria*, May 13, 1961, 93 (19), 5-8.

The problems of old age are many, but so are the blessings, if only the elderly know how to take advantage of them. Suggestions are made to enhance the prayer life of elderly persons in a way that will make their existence more meaningful.

457. Thompson, Gjermund. The rights of older persons—to share the faith. *Lutheran Social Concern*, Summer 1972, *12* (2), 46-47.

The witness of the older person issues from decades of experience with his own fumblings and uncertainties, his defeats and his victories. His witness is evidence of how he has responded to God's dealings with him through these decades. His retirement does not imply that he has vacated the world; his faith still pushes him into concern for all. The need of the world is for an affirmation of God's nearness and relevance in Jesus Christ: the older person responds to that need.

458. Thompson, William D. Pastoral implications of environmental control in mitigating senility in the aged. *Journal of Pastoral Counseling*, Fall-Winter 1976, *11*, 42-53.

The prognosis for "senility" (understood here as emotional breakdowns in elderly people) becomes more favorable in relation to age, the control of the physical and social environment, as well as control of the nonmaterial environment. The underlying theology in considering the potential implications of environmental control in mitigating senility in the aged is a theology of community: strong support from other persons.

459. Tracy, David. Eschatological perspectives on aging. In Hiltner, Seward (Ed.), *Toward a theology of aging*. New York: Human Sciences Press, 1975, pp. 119-34. NB: Also found in *Pastoral Psychology*, Winter 1975, *24*, 119-34.

(Citation 459 continued)

The reality of aging is a concrete expression of experiencing ourselves as temporal beings. The analysis appeals to a philosophical interpretation of temporality and a Christian theological interpretation of eschatology. Three eschatological symbol systems are noted: the traditional (past-oriented), the prophetic (present-oriented), and the apocalyptic (future oriented). These symbols should orient us in a positive way toward the process of aging.

460. Trese, Leo.   Our last years are the greatest: Vocation of prayer. *Sign,* September 1963, *42,* 32.

Suggests that the fetish of independence, of "not being a burden to anyone" in one's later years, is a self-defeating mirage. Unless we die young, we inevitably become dependent on others. Eventually bodily resources will become too attenuated to do anything but sit. The last years can also be the most useful years: contemplative, prayerful, bringing grace.

461. Townsend, Dorothy.   When Sisters retire, it's work, work, work. *Catholic Digest,* December 1972, *37,* 89-92.

The habits of a lifetime are hard to break, so the point is made that Sisters stay very active in retirement. (Note: The "Sisters" are nuns, women belonging to a religious order or community.)

462. Vega, Sister Lucy Marie.   *An annotated bibliography on aging for members of religious communities and clergy.* Denton: North Texas State University Center for Studies in Aging, August 1979, typescript.

This bibliography was compiled with a view to enhancing the retirement years of clergy and members of Catholic religious congregations. Its five chapters group entries under the headings of "Aging and Religious Life," "Religious Life and Retirement," "The Spiritual Dimension of Aging," "Training for Second Careers," "Health and Leisure." Included are books, articles, newspapers, audio-visual materials, and unpublished materials.

463. Vinson, Ann.   The role of religion in the maturation of the autonomous older adult. In Thorson, James A., & Cook, Thomas C., Jr., *Spiritual well-being of the elderly.* Springfield, Ill.: Charles C. Thomas, 1980, 127-33.

"By exercising spiritual faculties and perception, a higher concept of God is obtained. . . . The later years can be filled with creativity. . . . Until spiritual well-being becomes the rule and not the exception, aging will continue to be an artifact of our philosophical environment, a concept formed artificially by an industrial society, medical and genetic theory and social and psychological experimentation."

464. Voris, John R.   Let senior citizens serve others. *Christian Century,* March 2, 1960, *77* (9), 215-53.

(Citation 464 continued)

This article expresses dissatisfaction with the way the church is responding to the challenge of the elderly. Programs and projects are not enough; the churches must recognize the moral values involved with the place of the aged in our society. In sermons, conversations, and classes, ministers should direct elderly persons' attention outside themselves, to see their duty as a functioning, witnessing Christian.

465. Voris, John R.   Retirement homes: Untapped resources. *Christian Century*, February 21, 1962, 79 (8), 226-28.

Talented, financially able residents of Protestant, church-directed homes need to become an ecumenical, socially oriented force for good in the community, fostering ethical and social ideals. They can be benefactors of society, as well as its beneficiaries.

466. Ward, Sister Mary Cecilia.   Planning for a short future. *Sisters Today*, March 1974, *45*, 389-93.

For everyone there comes a time to consider what is the best way to spend the future. In religious communities, plans for the management of retired members seem to be proliferating. The elderly Sister needs to remain busy and interested, to grow in her prayer life. For some Sisters a "second career" may be the right thing.

467. Waterman, Leroy.   Religion and religious observance in old age. In Tibbitts, Clark (Ed.), *Living through the older years*. Ann Arbor: Univ. of Michigan Press, 1949, 99-112.

Only in the last two pages of this 14-page chapter does the writer discuss the aging and their religion. What precedes is his reflection about religion in general and Christianity in particular. Even on pages 110-12, the religion of the aging is only mentioned, not really examined. The wording of his title seemed to promise much more.

468. White House Conference on Aging (1961), Committee on Religion and Aging.   (Co-Chairmen, Raymond J. Gallagher; Marc H. Tannenbaum; William J. Villaume.) *Background paper on services of religious groups for the aging.* Washington, D.C.: U.S. Govt. Printing Office, 1960.

[See entry under Part 2 of this bibliography, "Gallagher-Tannenbaum-Villaume," for background paper #15 setting forth the philosophy and background paper #20 listing various services provided.]

469. (White House Conference on Aging) Special Staff on Aging HEW.   *Religion and aging. Reports and guidelines for the White House Conference on Aging.* Washington, D.C.: U.S. Govt. Printing Office, 1961.

Title self-explanatory.

470. White House Conference on Aging, National Planning Board. *Work book on spiritual well-being.* Washington, D.C.: U.S. Govt. Printing Office, 1971.

Part 1: Background. What do we mean by spiritual? spiritual needs of the elderly, what promotes spiritual well-being? the role of religion, influence of religion, role of religious organizations, role of community and government agencies, deficiencies of present programs. Part 2: Issues. Underlying assumptions are stated, and four issues are proposed in the form of questions.

471. White House Conference on Aging 1971. *Recommended for action: Facilities, programs, services.* Washington, D.C.: U.S. Govt. Printing Office, 1972.

This booklet contains only one paragraph that has anything to do with religion: "The government should cooperate with religious organizations and concerned social and educational agencies to provide research and professional training in matters of spiritual well-being to those who deliver services to the aging."

472. White House Conference on Aging 1971. *Recommended for action: Training.* Washington, D.C.: U.S. Govt. Printing Office, 1972.

Religion is mentioned several times under the heading of "Spiritual Well-being," on pages 5-6 and 8. There is some repetition. Another paragraph relevant to our topic is "Religious Community and Aging," page 6.

473. Wimberly, Anne Streaty. Configurational patterns in the function of the church for aging persons: A black perspective. *Journal of the International Theological Center,* Spring 1979, 6, 94-105.

The first impression of this article is one of academic jargon, replete with such terms as role enactment, group regard, and configurational patterns. All of this occupies half of the article. Beginning on page 100, mention is made of studying ten Black Protestant churches in the metropolitan Atlanta area. "Collection of data was accomplished through focused interviews with the pastors of the ten churches. Thus, the survey was limited to the clergy's knowledge and observations about the aged constituency and parishioner attitudes." Ten roles are identified, ranging from leader to worker. It was felt that half of the churches studied had achieved an acceptable balance between the young and the aged; in the rest; it was considered problematic. Suggestions are offered for further research.

SUPPLEMENT
TITLES WITHOUT ANNOTATION

The first part of this section includes titles that could not be located. The second part includes titles acquired while the main sections were in production. These titles are included in the Subject and Author Indices.

Unlocated titles

474. Abad Leon, F. Assistencia religiosa domiciliaria del anciano. (Ministry to the elderly in their own homes.) *Revista Española de Gerontologia*, 1972, 7, 223-30.

475. App, Austin. The later years: A spiritual opportunity. *Crosier*, February 1961, 36, 26-32.

476. Cooney, C. J. *The specialization of religious care of the elderly.* Denton: North Texas State Univ. Aging Studies, 1973.

477. Join with older adults in Christian fellowship. Nashville: Methodist Church General Board of Education, Department of the Christian Education of Adults, 1957.

478. Maziers. La place des personnes âgées dans les communautés de croyants. (Position of the elderly in communities of believers.) *Revue de Gérontologie d'Expression Française (Paris)*, 1974, 3 (6), 24; 27-28.

479. Moss, Steven A. Aging, death, and God. *Archives of the Foundation of Thanatology*, 1978, 7 (2), 24.

480. Odenwald, R. Catholics and old age. *Guild of Catholic Psychiatrists' Bulletin*, July 1963, 10, 181-85.

481. Oles, E. S. *Religion and old age: A study of the possible influence of religious adherence on adjustment.* (Thesis.) Lewisburg, Pa.: Bucknell University, 1949.

482. Seminaries and aging. National Retired Teachers Association/American Association of Retired Persons. Mimeo, n.d.

483. Starting an older adult group in your church. Nashville: Methodist Church General Board of Education, Department of the Christian Education of Adults, 1956.

484. Yost, Donald. *Report on a pilot project on aging in Westmoreland Co., Penn.* Greensburg, Pa: First Lutheran Church, n.d.

New titles

485. Buchen, Irving H. An introduction to future scenarios: The issue of the elderly. *Church and Society*, January-February 1980, 70, 41-47.

486. Clements, William M. Reminiscence as the cure of souls in early old age. *Journal of Religious Health*, Spring 1981, 20, 41-47.

487. Dahlstrom, Earl C. Toward a theology of aging. *Covington Quarterly*, February 1979, 37, 3-15.

488. Delloff, Linda M. Democracy in action and inaction [1981 White House Conference on Aging; editorial]. *Christian Century*, December 16, 1981, 98, 1299-1300.

114

SUPPLEMENT

489. Delloff, Linda M. Mr. Barclay goes to Washington: Religion at the White House Conference on Aging. *Christian Century*, December 30, 1981, 98, 1363-66.

490. Hubbard, Richard W. Pastoral care in the nursing home: Guidelines for communication with institutionalized elderly. *Journal of Pastoral Care*, December 1979, 33, 239-42.

491. Keeley, Benjamin J. Generations in tension: Intergenerational differences and continuities in religion and religion-related behavior. *Review of Religious Research*, Spring 1976, 17, 221-31.

492. Meiburg, Albert L. Conference on aging: realistic expectation. *Christian Century*, November 11, 1981, 98, 1151-52.

493. Mohring, Martha J. Convalescent homes: Places for ministry. *Christianity Today*, December 11, 1981, 25, 70.

494. United Presbyterian Church in the U.S.A. Ministry to and with aging persons [document]. *Church and Society*, July-August 1981, 71, 29-40.

495. Ziegler, Jesse H. (Ed.) Education for ministry in aging: Gerontology in seminary training. *Theological Education*, Winter 1980 (Special issue No. 3), 16, 271-414.

●

496. Aging in the eighties: E/SA Forum 72. *Engage/Social Action*, June 1981, 9, 9-40.

497. Glick, Ruth. Older Americans: A resource for continuing contributions. *Engage/Social Action*, June 1981, 9, 10-12.

498. Jewish Association for Services for the Aged. *GeronTopics for the Aging Network* (1982), 5, 12.

499. Kaiser, Marvin A.; Peters, George R.; Babchuk, Nicholas. When priests retire. *Gerontologist*, February 1982, 22, 89-94.

500. Mickelsen, Alvera. To honor your parents: The chance for a lifetime. *Christianity Today*, 1981, 25, 791-95.

501. Minnery, Tom. Christian retirement homes: A rest along the way. *Christianity Today*, 1981, 25, 583-86.

502. Snyder, Ross. An enterprise of transgenerational adulthood: "we did it this way." *The Christian Ministry*, July 1981, 12, 5-14.

503. Snyder, Ross. Religious meaning and the latter third of life. *Religious Education*, September-October 1981, 76, 534-52.

504. Surrey, Peter J. Until she dies [nursing homes]. *Christian Ministry*, July 1981, 12, 31-33.

SUBJECT

Note: The following reference numbers indicate the *number of the entry*. A small letter "d" following a number means that this particular entry offered data based on some sort of measurement. Local communities mentioned in entries are indexed by state.

Adjustment, personal, 7d, 34d, 46d, 47, 59, 70, 71, 72d, 73d, 74d, 75d, 76d, 81d, 86d, 89d, 90d, 91d, 481
Afterlife, 1, 9, 58d, 95, 104d
Anabaptist, 29d
Attitude, religious, 88, 96
Attitudes toward the aged, 217d, 247, 248, 292, 293, 307
Baptist church: American, 292d, 293d; Southern, 170, 212, 240, 284, 454
Black aged, 34d, 43, 54, 132d, 408, 473
California, 41, 129, 145, 180, 189, 192, 220
Canada, 134
Catholic, Roman, 3, 18d, 33d, 38d, 57d, 96d, 108d, 121, 122, 124, 125, 131, 133, 134, 135, 138, 139, 142, 143, 144, 145, 146, 148, 149, 150, 155, 156, 162, 163, 165, 168, 169, 172, 185, 187, 192, 197, 198, 199, 200, 201, 209, 214, 224, 231, 234, 236, 238, 257, 282, 291, 317, 318, 321, 325, 341, 390, 393, 394, 396, 397, 398, 404, 417, 419, 433, 442, 450, 462, 480, 499d
Church attendance. *See* Religious practice in old age
Church of Christ, 349
Clergymen, aged, 84, 388, 411, 417, 420
Colorado, 175
Commitment, religious, 39d, 83d, 103
Congregational church, 42
Connecticut, 234
Counseling, 244, 250, 265, 335, 365, 401, 421
Dignity, 26, 120, 423, 435
Disciples of Christ church, 184, 309, 354, 355d
Disengagement and religion, 30, 69, 84, 393
Duke University longitudinal study, 15d, 16d, 52
Ecumenism, 363, 372
Episcopal church. *See* Protestant Episcopal church
Faith development stage, 98, 99, 410
Families, 79, 118, 122, 137, 249, 259, 328, 345, 348, 358, 500
Florida, 30, 202, 215, 240, 265, 320
Fear of death, 58, 67, 68d, 87d, 93, 95, 103, 106, 111, 113
France, 142, 242, 291, 478
Georgia, 240, 473
German, 18, 29
Germany, 163, 164, 437
Hawaii, 332
Homes for the aged, 3d, 12d, 63d, 89-92, 124, 127, 148, 153, 156, 157, 171, 175, 191, 203, 222, 239, 240, 258, 269, 274, 294, 317, 318, 337, 341, 357, 363, 386, 465, 490, 493, 501, 504
Hospitals, 83, 339, 362
Illinois, 14, 46, 86
Importance of religion to the aged, 6, 10, 19d, 20, 25d, 28, 29d, 31, 32, 82d, 447, 463
Indiana, 4, 107, 405, 419
Institutionalization. *See* Homes for the aged
Integration of older members, 183, 379. *See also* Segregation of the elderly
Interaction theory, 393
Intergenerational differences, 491
Iowa, 166
Japan, 258
Jewish aged, 33d, 43, 60, 62d, 99, 115, 124, 127, 167, 171, 179, 226, 235, 239, 282, 313, 338, 340, 376, 378, 392, 395, 408, 409, 448, 449, 498
Kentucky, 240
Knights of Columbus, 213
La Vie Montante, 242, 291, 366
Life review, 98, 486

Life satisfaction, 1, 17d, 37d, 38d, 54, 55d, 101d, 180
Longevity, 9, 10, 127, 281
Louisiana, 154, 220
Lutheran, 29d, 53d, 118, 208, 333, 346, 357, 407, 441, 457, 484; attitudes of church members towards aged, 217d; American, 120; hospital, 362; in America (LCA), 160, 174; National Lutheran Council, 186; social service system, 116, 186, 206, 215; United, 344
Maryland, 105, 195
Massachusetts, 115
Methodist church. *See* United Methodist church
Metropolitan areas, 13, 14, 33
Michigan, 85, 162, 201, 232, 404
Ministry with or to older members, 40, 41, 160, 170, 188, 228, 240d, 253, 255, 256, 260, 264, 267, 270, 271, 272, 278, 279, 284, 292, 302, 309, 312, 314, 315, 316, 323, 324, 325, 328, 329, 331, 336, 342, 345, 413, 429, 432, 435, 443, 463
Minnesota, 70-75, 106, 131, 162, 333
Missouri, 69, 123, 161, 165, 200, 213, 219, 325
National Interfaith Coalition on Aging, 1, 288, 372, 373, 454
National Council on the Aging, 82, 431
Needs: of the aging (general), 14, 35, 40, 41, 50, 64, 102, 149, 153, 154, 158, 162, 180, 181d, 182, 228, 255, 283d, 290, 333, 335, 368, 383, 400, 401, 405, 406, 413, 414, 426, 427, 452; spiritual, 35, 80, 127, 129, 130
Nevada, 189
New Mexico, 240, 304
New York, 18, 63, 124, 125, 126, 143, 148, 157, 162, 185, 187, 197, 220, 238, 308, 421
North Carolina, 16
Nuns, 65, 200, 207, 221, 375, 381, 391, 393, 394, 396, 397, 398, 404, 406, 416, 433, 442, 461, 466
Ohio, 40, 108, 139, 162, 211
Oklahoma, 220
Oregon, 419
Pain, 315d
Pennsylvania, 29, 171, 172, 218, 349, 484
Presbyterian church, 40, 157, 181d, 182, 295, 303d, 337; Presbyterian Church in U.S., 194, 286; Presbyterian Church in U.S.A., 203, 204; United Presbyterian Church in U.S.A., 137, 218, 228, 229, 377, 494
Programs for the aged, 40, 124, 128, 131, 141, 143, 145, 154, 158, 162, 164, 165, 167, 172, 173, 175, 178, 180, 194, 195, 202, 204, 208, 210, 212, 218, 220, 229, 235, 239, 271, 273, 275, 298, 304, 309, 340, 371, 386, 421
Protestant, 15d, 16d, 29d, 33d, 68d, 89-92, 96d, 153, 177, 211, 220, 282, 300, 437, 465
Protestant Episcopal church, 45, 195, 319, 413
Quakers (Friends), 205
Reformed church, 29
Religion and aging, relationship between, 7d, 11, 422
Religious belief in old age, 9, 23d, 55d
Religious disaffiliation, 6
Religious education of older people, 177, 181, 182, 188, 255, 294, 303d, 322, 414, 415, 437
Religious practice in old age, 4d, 6d, 10, 24d, 33d, 39d, 40d, 42d, 48d, 55d, 57d, 61d, 78, 79, 81, 82d, 85d, 86d, 101d, 104d, 107d, 112d
Retirement, 51, 84, 117, 221, 243, 249, 251, 252, 285, 335, 366, 377, 383, 385, 387, 388, 394, 397,

404, 411, 417, 420, 424, 430, 438, 442, 444, 445, 449, 461, 462, 465, 466, 499d.
Role of the church/synagogue, 41, 119, 137, 176, 189, 190, 237, 296, 315, 352, 363, 371, 380, 383, 385, 401, 405, 421, 427, 429, 436, 445, 452
Rural areas, 8, 13
Salvation army, 210
Scotland, 96
Segregation of the elderly, 343. *See also* Integration of older members
Seminaries, 161, 182, 264, 305, 337, 359, 482, 495; seminarians, 339
Services provided by the churches, 119, 122, 123, 128, 139, 146, 147, 162, 166, 167, 186, 189, 190, 195, 196, 206, 213, 229, 360, 363, 371, 374, 413, 441
Seventh-Day Adventists, 180
Social aspects of religion, 2d, 4d
Social issues, 36
South Carolina, 240
Spirituality and aging, 216, 254, 266, 268, 285, 297, 369, 384, 407, 418, 434, 451, 460, 462
St. Vincent de Paul Society, 139, 196, 232, 233, 273, 440
Suggestions, from aged persons, 41, 253, 296, 327, 337, 348, 350, 455, 464

Terman Group interest in religion, 66d
Texas, 182, 223, 286, 446
Theology of aging, 7, 21, 137, 158, 161, 218, 259, 285, 289, 324, 356, 361, 379, 399, 403, 439, 448, 459, 487
Training of clergy, 259, 264, 265, 267, 305, 306, 319, 320, 326, 333, 337, 359, 373
Union of American Hebrew Congregations, 226
Unitarian Universalist, 227, 343
United Methodist church, 89, 119, 222, 225, 275, 302, 365, 453, 477, 483, 496, 497
United Church of Christ, 307, 349
Visitors and visiting of aged, 128, 143, 162, 206, 255, 256, 269, 273, 275, 276, 293, 301, 311, 326, 330, 344, 421
Volunteers, 234, 257, 321, 347
Washington, 39
Washington, D.C., 319
White House Conference on Aging: of 1961, 146, 151, 395, 468, 469; of 1971, 373, 428, 431, 470-472; of 1981, 372, 373, 488, 489, 492
Widowhood, 13
Wisconsin, 173, 236
Women, 35, 91, 92, 94, 99, 104, 167, 192
Work as affecting religion, 51d, 243

AUTHOR

Abad Leon, F., 474
Abraams, Edith, 115
Adams, Davis L., 1
Adkins, Paul Russell, 240
Ailor, James W., 119
Albers, Thomas L., 241
Albrecht, Ruth E., 2, 448
Allix, Robert, 242
Alston, Jon P. 112
Amen, Sister M. Ann, 3
Andrews, G. R., 96
Angus, Jack Duane, 4
Ankenbrandt, Thomas, 350
Apfeldorf, Max, 5
App, Austin J., 121, 475
Argyle, Michael, 351
Armstrong, Priscilla, 243
Armstrong, Robert, 243
Au, Thomas Hardy, 352
Babbie, Earl R., 45
Babchuk, Nicholas, 499
Bahr, Howard M., 6
Baptista, Sister Maria, 122
Barozzi, Al, 353
Barron, Milton L., 7, 448
Bashford, Anthony, 244
Basset, Joseph A., 8
Batzka, David L., 354, 355
Baumgartner, I., 113
Beard, Belle B., 9, 10
Beattie, Walter M., 123, 137
Becker, Arthur H., 245
Becker, K. F., 11, 356
Bell, Tony, 12
Bellerose, Sister Yvette, 216
Belter, E. W., 357
Bennett, John C., 259
Bently, Virgil, 246
Berardo, Felix M., 13
Bernholz, Adolph, 358
Berman, Rochel, 124
Bernadette de Lourdes, Mother
   Mary, 125
Bier, Wiliam C., 126
Bild, Bernice, 14
Biller, Newman M., 127
Blakely, Thomas J., 128
Blazer, Dan G., 15, 16
Blizzard, Samuel L., 360, 448
Boe, Paul A., 362
Böckle, Franz, 361
Boeddeker, Alfred, 129
Bortner, Rayman W., 17
Botz, Paschal, 247, 248
Bower, Janet, 18
Braceland, Francis, 137
Braun, Viola K., 130
Brekke, Milo L., 53
Brennan, Constance L., 19
Brigh, Sister Mary, 131
Brink, T. L., 249
Brown, J. Paul, 250
Brown, Philip S., 20
Browning, Don S., 21
Buchen, Irving H., 485
Buesching, Sister Rosaria, 22
Butler, Clarence, 251
Butler, Robert, 363
Buxbaum, Robert E., 252
Caird, F. I., 96
Cale, W. Franklin, 253
Caligiuri, Angelo M., 216, 254
Cameron, Paul, 132

Campbell, Oscar P., 255
Cantellon, John E. 444
Carlson, Paul, 256
Castellan, F. H. W., 258
Chakerian, Charles G., 137
Chamouland, Muriel, 205
Christiansen, Drew, 26, 117
Clements, William M., 259, 365,
   486
Clingan, Donald, 27, 260
Cody, John Cardinal, 138
Coffy, Archbishop Robert, 366
Cole, Elbert, 28, 259
Cole, Spurgeon, 111
Collier, Charlotte Meier, 29
Connolly, Kathleen, 117
Cook, C. J., 139
Cook, John William, 30
Cook, Thomas C. Jr., 109, 140,
   261
Cooney, C. J., 476
Cottrell, Fred, 367
Covalt, Nila Kirkpatrick, 31, 32,
   448
Cowhig, James D., 33
Creen, Edward, 368
Cryns, Arthur G., 308
Culver, Elsie Thomas, 141
Cunningham, Sister Agnes, 369
Dahlstrom, Earl C., 487
Dancy, Joseph Jr., 34
Darlington, Charles, 205
Davidson, Norman L., 370
Davis, David C., 262
Davis, Jack A., 371
Defois, Gérard, 142
Delloff, Linda M., 372, 373,
   488, 489
Demmy, Michael, 143
Deneen, Sister Francis Mary, 263
Desmond, Thomas C., 374
Devaney, Donald, 375
DeWolf, Rose, 136
Donovan, Harlow, 35
Dortzbach, Elmer, 264
Douglas, Margaret, 145
Dowd, J. J., 36
Drapela, Victor J., 265
Duckat, Walter, 376
Dunn, Patricia, 266
Dunne, Agnese, 377
Edwards, John N., 37
Engelsberg, Rega, 205
Entman, Sidney, 378, 448
Ewing, James W., 259
Eymard, Sister M., 131
Fahey, Charles, 117, 268, 379,
   380, 412, 442
Faist, Russell L., 146
Faunce, Frances Avery, 269
Fecher, Con J., 381, 433
Ferenstein, Barbara Collins, 147
Ferguson, Larry N., 38
Finney, John M., 39
Fischer, Edward, 382
Fitch, William C., 383
Flemming, Arthur S., 446
Foley, James, 384
Ford, Robert A., 148
Ford, Steven R., 270
Foster, Lloyd, 385
Fournier, William OMI, 271
Fox, Alfred, 41, 272

Frakes, Margaret, 386
Frautschi, Barbara, 40
Freeman, Eileen, 193
Frommelt, H., 387
Fukuyama, Yashia, 42
Gaffney, Sister Marie, 149, 442
Gaffney, Walter J., 434
Gallagher, Raymond, 150, 151,
   468
Gariboldi, Ronald John, 274
Geis, Ellen, 124
Gilmore, Anne J. J., 96
Gitelman, Paul J., 43
Gleason, George, 153
Glick, Ruth, 497
Glock, Charles Y., 44, 45
Goetz, Howard C. Jr., 154
Goodling, Richard A., 275
Gorry, Edward, 117, 388
Gratton, Carolyn, 389
Gray, Robert M., 46, 47
Greene, Padraig, 276
Guinan, Sister St. Michael, 391
Guttmann, David, 392
Hafrey, Daniel J., 157
Hammond, Phillip E., 277
Hamovitch, Maurice B., 444
Harrington, Janette, 158
Harris, Thomas A., 278
Hartman, Grover, 405
Hashian, Lorraine, 412
Havighurst, Robert, 14
Heenan, Edward F., 49, 393
Heinecken, Martin, 160, 259
Hellerich, Ralph, 160
Helminiak, Daniel A., 266
Herold, Sister Duchesne, 394
Hershey, Lenore, 136
Heschel, Abraham, 395
Hickey, Thomas, 396, 397, 398
Hiltner, Seward, 161, 399, 400,
   448
Hixenbaugh, Elinor R., 162
Hoeffner, J. Cardinal, 163
Hofmeister, G., 164
Hogan, William F., 401
Holbrook, T., 402
Hollopeter, Herchel, 405
Holmes, Urban T., 259
Hougland, Kenneth, 279
Hover, Margot K., 165
Howie, Carl G., 403
Hubbard, Richard W., 490
Hultsch, David F., 17
Hunter, Woodrow, 404
Hustedde, Sister Germaine, 216
Ingraham, M. H., 50
Jacobs, H. Lee, 166
Jacobs, Ruth H., 51
Jacobs, William J., 456
Jean, Sister Gabrielle L., 406
Jeffers, Frances C., 52
John Paul II, 168, 169, 280, 281
John XXIII, 280, 281, 451
Johnson, Arthur L., 53
Johnson, Gerald K., 407
Johnson, Lois Mary, 54
Johnson, Marilyn E., 55
Johnson, Murray C., 205
Johnson, Richard, 288
Jungkuntz, Daniel, 282
Kader, Raymond A., 170
Kaiser, Marvin A., 499

Kalish, Richard A., 397, 398
Kalson, Leon, 171
Kanouse-Roberts, Aliça, 408
Katz, Robert L., 409
Keeley, Benjamin J., 491
Keith, Pat M., 283
Kerr, Horace, 284
Kerschner, Paul, 442
Kilduff, Thomas, 285
Kimble, Melvin A., 259
King, J. Carter III, 182, 286
Kitson, Gay C., 293
Kivett, Vira R., 56
Kleban, Morton H., 60
Klemmack, David L., 37
Knapp, Kenneth R., 287, 412
Knierim, Rolf, 259
Knox, Margaret, 448
Knoy, Zane, 288
Kohlberg, Lawrence, 410
Kragnes, Earl N., 289
Krawinkel, Robert, 282
Kuhlen, Raymond G., 57, 444
Kurlychek, Robert T., 58
LaFarge, John, 411
Lamb, R. Ernest, 205
Lampe, M. Willard, 290
Laporte, Jean, 259
Larue, Gerald A., 59
Lawton, M. Powell, 60
Lazenby, Herbert, 137
Lazerwitz, Bernard, 61
Lebowitz, Barry P., 62
Lee, Gary R., 39
Lee, William M., 172
Legan, Kathryn, 173
Lepkowski, J. Richard, 63
Leport, Father (no first name given), 291
Linstrom, Robert C., 219
Londoner, Carroll A., 414
Longino, Charles F. Jr., 292, 293
Lopata, Helen Znaniecki, 310
Lott, J., 415
Lovely, Sister Marie Laurette, 416
Lucas, G., 36
Lynch, Philip Arthur, 294
McAloon, Brian, 193
McAuliffe, Dismas, 117
McCarthy, Johanna E., 412
McCarty, Shaun, 418
McClellan, Robert W., 295
McDowell, John, 64, 137
McGinty, Donna L., 261
McGreevy, Sister Mary Virginia, 419
MacGuigan, J. E., 417
McIsaac, Sister Mary Trinita, 65
McKeon, Richard M., 296
McNally, Arthur, 297
McNeill, Don, 312
Madden, Declan, 175
Maesen, William A., 412
Malony, H. Newton, 38
Manno, Bruno V., 298
Marino, Robert, 299
Marshall, Helen, 66
Martin, David, 67, 68
Marty, Martin E., 259
Masse, Benjamin, 420
Mathiasen, Grace, 421
Maves, Paul B., 176, 177, 178, 300, 301, 385, 422
Maxwell, Jack M., 182

Maziers, 478
Meiburg, Albert L., 492
Meier, Levi, 179
Menkin, Eva L., 423
Mershon, James Merwyn, 180
Mickelsen, Alvera, 500
Miller, Donald E., 259
Mills, B. M., 181
Mills, Beatrice Marie, 303
Mindel, Charles H., 69
Minnery, Tom, 501
Missinne, Leo E., 19
Moberg, David O., 47, 70-81, 183, 305, 306, 424-429, 444
Moberg, Richard Gordon, 307
Moeller, Walter H., 260
Mohring, Martha J., 493
Monk, Abraham, 308
Montgomery, J. Dexter, 309
Moore, Allen, 259
Morcyz, Richard K., 216
Morgan, John H., 310, 430
Mosely, J. Edward, 184
Moss, Steven A., 479
Mulanaphy, J. M., 50
Murphy, Joseph, 185
Murphy, Sister Patricia, 311
Naus, Peter, 312, 432
Nelson, Franklyn L., 83
Ng, David, 182, 188
Nichols, Claude R., 52
Nix, James T., 381, 433
Norris, Arthur H., 105
Nouwen, Henri J. M., 312, 434
Novick, Louis J., 313
Nugent, Frank McGill, 84
O'Collins, Gerald, 216
O'Connell, Patrick, 435
Odenwald, R., 480
Odom, Melita, 66
O'Donnell, P., 191
Ogle, Alice, 192
Oglesby, William B. Jr., 310, 314
Oles, E. S., 481
O'Malley, Sarah OSB, 271
Orbach, Harold L., 85
O'Reilly, Charles T., 86
O'Rourke, William D., 87
Packard, George F., 195
Palmore, Erdman B., 15, 16, 88
Pan, Ju-Shu, 89, 90, 91, 92
Papa, Mary Baker, 436
Paterson, George, 259
Pattie, Alice M., 405
Payne, Barbara Pittard, 93, 259, 315
Peacock, Richard L., 316
Peralta, V., 117, 136, 198, 199
Peters, George R., 499
Phillips, Ambrose, K., 317, 318
Pistrui, William, 200
Pitrone, Jean Madden, 201
Poehlmann, H. G., 437
Poteat, Gordon, 202, 448
Pruyser, Paul W., 439
Query, Joy M., 94
Quinn, Philip F., 320
Randall, Ollie, 385
Rank, Betty Jane, 321
Rasmussen, Will C., 206
Reboul, Hélène, 95
Regan, Thomas F., 440

Reichert, Richard, 322
Reichert, Sara, 322
Reid, W. S., 96
Reisch, Harold W., 323, 441
Ringer, Benjamin B., 45
Rismiller, Arthur P., 208
Robb, Thomas Bradley, 324, 443
Robinson, Barry, 117
Rodney, Bernard, 209
Rogers, Tommy, 97
Rosenthal, Rudolph M., 405
Rost, Robert Anthony, 325
Rowe, Gard Linwood, 326
Ruhbach, G., 327
Runions, J. E., 328
Sandven, Joe Morris, 445
Sauer, Stephen F., 446
Saxon, S. J., 139
Scarborough, Bernard, 341
Schaller, Lyle E., 211
Schnore, Leo F., 33
Schumacher, Henry C., 447, 448
Scudder, Delton L., 448
Seitz, M., 329
Semancik, Joseph, 330
Sessoms, Robert L., 212
Shapero, Sanford M., 449
Shulik, Richard Norman, 98
Sidney, Waltar, 299
Siefert, Brother E., 450
Siegel, Lawrence, 282
Siegel, Martha Kaufer, 99
Simmons, Henry, 368
Singer, Maurice, 60
Singh, Kripal, 100
Singleton, Albert, 213
Sloyan, Virginia, 117
Smith, Bert Kruger, 182, 331
Smith, R., 451
Smith, Theodore Kurtz, 332
Snyder, Eldon E., 101
Snyder, Ross, 502, 503
Soete, Catherine J., 214
Spencer, Sue W., 137
Spreitzer, Elmer, 101
Springfield, T., 452
Stafford, Virginia, 102, 405, 453
Stagg, Frank, 454
Stainback, Berry, 136
Stamats, Esther C., 405, 455
Stadenmaier, Wilbert, 117
Stark, Rodney, 103
Steele, Paul E., 355
Steines, Meriel, 94
Steinitz, Lucy Y., 104
Stene, A. Marlin, 333
Stere, Patricia L., 217
Steury, Steven, 412
Stevenson, John Robert, 218
Stone, Jane Livermore, 105
Stough, Ada Barnett, 220, 444
Stout, Robert Joe, 334
Strain, Sister Rose Mary, 221, 442
Stressman, Roger, 222
Strom, Kenneth R., 335
Strommen, Merton, 53
Suedkamp, Wilbur E., 456
Surrey, Peter, 504
Svoboda, Robert, 336
Swaim, William T., 337
Swenson, Wendell M., 106, 444
Talley, Kay, 320
Tannenbaum, Marc H., 151, 468
Taves, Marvin J., 81

Taylor, Robert N. Jr., 339
Theisen, Sylvester, 107
Therese, Sister Mary, 108
Thompson, Gjermund, 457
Thompson, John, 224
Thompson, Prescott, 137
Thompson, William D., 458
Thorson, James A., 109
Tillock, Eugene E., 341
Tobiessen, Florence, 205
Townsend, Dorothy, 136, 461
Trachtenberg, Beth, 412
Tracy, David, 459
Trese, Leo, 460
Trifiro, Anthony, 143
Ulanov, Ann Belford, 259
Underwager, Ralph C., 53
Underwood, Ralph L., 182, 342

Upton, Lawrence, 137
Van Boening, Gary Don, 345
Varga, Andrew, 117
Vaughan, C. Edwin, 69
Vega, Sister Lucy Marie, 462
Villaume, William J., 151, 468
Vinson, Ann, 463
Voris, John R., 464, 465
Wahlstrom, Catherine Lee, 233
Walker, Gladys H., 234
Walters, Frank J., 185
Ward, Sister Mary Cecilia, 466
Waterman, Leroy, 110, 467
Watson, Harriet, 136
Webb, Muriel S., 158
Wegesa, Benjamin, 205
Weisman, Celia B., 235
Wheelock, Robert D., 237, 310

Whitehead, James D., 259
Whitehead, Evelyn Eaton, 259
Wiederaenders, Ruth, 346
Williams, Robert L., 111
Wimberly, Anne Streaty, 473
Wingrove, C. Ray, 112
Wittkowski, J., 113
Wood, Vivian, 412
Wrightsman, Lawrence S. Jr., 67, 68
Wygal, Winnifred, 347
Wynn, John Charles, 348
Wygant, W. E., 114
Yost, Donald, 484
Zenns, William C., 238
Ziegler, Jesse H., 495
Zoot, Vicki A., 239